Upward

Upward

Faith, Church, and the Ascension of Christ

Anthony J. Kelly, CSsR

A Michael Glazier Book

LITURGICAL PRESS
Collegeville, Minnesota

www.litpress.org

A Michael Glazier Book published by Liturgical Press

Cover design by Jodi Hendrickson. Cover photo: Dreamstime.

1   2   3   4   5   6   7   8   9

Library of Congress Cataloging-in-Publication Data

Kelly, Anthony, 1938–
    Upward : faith, church, and the Ascension of Christ / Anthony J. Kelly, CSSR.
        pages cm
    "A Michael Glazier book."
    Includes bibliographical references.
    ISBN 978-0-8146-8267-8 — ISBN 978-0-8146-8292-0 (ebook)
    1. Jesus Christ—Ascension.   2. Catholic Church—Doctrines.   I. Title.
BT500.K45   2014
232.9'7—dc23   2013045668

Contents

Preface

I began thinking about the ascension in the course of writing a previous study on the resurrection.[1] Like several others, I was seeking to remedy the comparative neglect of the resurrection in theology while acknowledging the magnificent contributions of writers such as Francois Durrwell, CSsR, and Gerald O'Collins, SJ, and learning much from the more recent work of theologians such as N. T. Wright. My particular approach was considerably influenced by modern French phenomenology as represented by Jean-Luc Marion, Claude Romano, and Michel Henry.

To make a long story short, I thought that there was much to be gained from a theology of the resurrection by treating it as a "saturated phenomenon," that is, an event and experience overbrimming any attempt to exhaust its meaning and control its influence. More positively still, such a phenomenon is ever-productive in the life of faith and in the mission of the church; indeed, its effect reaches into every aspect of reality and affects the course and outcome of human history.

My book was generally well received; and, as far as it went, contributed to current theological discussion in this area. However, it slowly dawned on me that I had been neglecting what we call, rather generally, "the ascension." Like many others, I was taking for granted that what we mean by the ascension of Christ was implied in his resurrection—for the Father through the power of the Spirit has raised up his Son to be the form, source, and first fruits of creation transformed. Who would doubt it? Nonetheless, there is one weakness in that presumption—it takes for granted that we possess a rather full knowledge of what the resurrection is and what

---

[1] Anthony J. Kelly, *The Resurrection Effect: Transforming Christian Life and Thought* (Maryknoll, NY: Orbis Books, 2008).

it implies for Christ and "for us and our salvation." Consequently, the ascension seems merely to embroider the basic event and veer, to a somewhat embarrassing degree, in a mythological direction as a gravity-defying form of levitation.

Opposed to such a presumption are Luke's accounts of the ascension in his gospel and in the Acts of the Apostles. A magisterial treatment of these texts was offered over forty years ago by Gerhard Lohfink in his work *Die Himmelfahrt Jesu*. But there is more in the New Testament on the ascension than the Lukan account, even if it is not described in explicitly Lukan terms, and especially when theology begins to use a more phenomenological approach to the experience of faith. As I will suggest, John's gospel can be read as a presentation of the "ascending Jesus," sometimes in explicit terms (John 1:51; 3:13; 6:62; 17:11; 20:17). Other representative examples are the Pauline Captivity Epistles with their perspective on Christ crucified, risen, ascended, and receiving the name above all names, before whom all creation must bend the knee (Phil 2:9-10).

In a somewhat similar manner, the Letter to the Hebrews and the Book of Revelation invite their hearers and readers to consider the activities of the ascended Jesus. In Hebrews, Jesus has pierced the veil and lives now to make intercession for all who must follow him (Heb 10:19). In Revelation, the Lamb who was slain acts as the Lord of creation and history in his presence to the church in every place and in every age (see Rev 21:9).

Though it has its roots in the Lukan narrative of distinguishable events (resurrection and ascension), the ascension in this larger sense can profitably be related to the "ascensional" dynamism of Jesus' whole existence as the Gospel of John describes it, especially in his going to the Father "to prepare a place" for his followers (John 14:2). Likewise, in the Pauline writings, the ascension connotes the present state of Christ as filling all things and holding all things together. In the further perspectives offered by Revelation and Hebrews, there is a sense of the activities of the ascended One as pioneer, intercessor, and Lord of history and the church. This more expansive consideration of the ascension not only enhances its status as a mystery of faith and an article of the Creed, but also brings larger dimensions to any consideration of the resurrection itself as the event that made all the difference. It suggests how the resurrection of the crucified is indeed a "saturated phenomenon," overbrimming all understandings and opening into the infinities of God's creative love. It points to that "other dimension," the strange paradox contained in the com-patibility of Christ's presence and absence in the life of the church.

Oddly, there has not been a great deal written on the ascension—perhaps because it is regarded as too elevated a topic—and certainly not much of any great practical value. Still, as this book argues, the ascension does shape the limitless horizon of Christian life and its outreach in mission, always moving beyond, upwards, outwards, to Christ who already occupies every dimension of time and space. The ascension supplies its own oxygen to the catholicity of faith and enables it to breathe deeply in its awareness of "the boundless riches of Christ" (Eph 3:9). Christ has ascended to the realm of God from which the Spirit comes, and from which he himself will return. Furthermore, in his ascension, Christ is closest to believers in the here and now of their present lives. Because the crucified and risen One is ascended, he is not reduced to an ethereal abstraction, but is rather encountered as a living presence, accessible to all, in every age and in every place—contemporary and accessible in all that he is, was, and will be, in his words and deeds, in his life and mission, in his passion, death, and resurrection.

However taken for granted the ascension has become, however much it represents that forgotten dimension of faith unconfined by the categories, concepts, systems, and concerns of our mundane existence (even in the church), this book is written with the convic-tion that there are further riches to be discovered. In the words of Paul, since God has "raised us up with him and seated us with him in the heavenly places" (Eph 2.6), it befits the followers of Christ to "set [our] minds on the things that are above, not on things that are on earth, for [we] have died, and [our] life is hidden with Christ in God" (Col 3:2). Accordingly, faith strains forward to what lies ahead, following the apostle as he pressed on "toward the goal for the prize of the upward (lit.) call of God in Christ Jesus" (Phil 3:14).

I would like to acknowledge my indebtedness to Mary Coloe, PBVM, notable biblical scholar, for her encouragement and lynx-eyed detection of the typos and misspelling, as well as raising ques-tions of biblical interpretation at crucial points. I must also thank my colleague, Maeve Heaney, VDMF, for opening up new vistas for me in her recent book *Music as Theology: What Music Says about the Word*, even though it was too late for me to incorporate what I learned into my own book. I cannot but thank another generous colleague, Rev. Dr. Joseph Lam, for his expert suggestions, in patristic theology above all. Of course, Hans Christoffersen of Liturgical Press is inexhaustible in his editorial dedication. I realize it is hard to sell books on the ascension—a topic which inevitably suggests a vantage point somewhat removed from the mundane calculations essential in today's book market! I thank him for taking this risk and hope that it will bring an appropriate reward. My thanks, too, to Patrick McGowan, the copy editor who dealt with this manuscript with that particular blend of patience and precision so necessary in the delicate task of correcting the deficiencies of a wayward author.

Chapter 1

Jesus Ascends—
and a World of Questions

Theologically speaking, the ascension of Jesus Christ has, over the years, suffered a form of benign neglect compared to other aspects of Christian faith. This has made it vulnerable to mythic fantasies that do nothing for faith or theology. Because the ascension has received so little critical theological attention, it tends to become a victim of a free floating imagination so as to appear as a mytho-logical extravagance to the point where faith, reason, and language are somewhat embarrassed. This is not to say that there are some notable exceptions on which this present work gratefully relies.[1] Gerhard Lohfink's seminal biblical investigation into the distinc-tive Lukan treatment of the ascension was written over forty years

---

[1] For example, Douglas Farrow, *Ascension and Ecclesia: On the Significance of the Doctrine of the Ascension for Ecclesiology and Christian Cosmology* (Edinburgh: T. & T. Clark, 1999), and *Ascension Theology* (London: T. & T. Clark, 2011); José Granados, "The First Fruits of the Flesh and the First Fruits of the Spirit: The Mystery of the Ascension," *Communio* 38, no. 2 (Spring 2011): 6–38; Brian D. Robinette, *Grammars of Resurrection: A Christian Theology of Presence and Absence* (New York: Crossroad, 2009). For earlier influential works, see Karl Barth, *Church Dogmatics*, ed. G. W. Bromiley and T. F. Torrance, vol. 4 (Edinburgh: T. & T. Clark, 1956–77); J. G. Davies, *He Ascended into Heaven: A Study in the History of Doctrine* (London: Lutterworth Press, 1958); F. X. Durrwell, *The Resurrection: A Biblical Study*, trans. Rosemary Sheed (London and New York: Sheed and Ward, 1960); G. Martelet, *The Risen Christ and the Eucharistic World*, trans. René Hague, (New York: Seabury Press, 1976); Thomas F. Torrance, *Space, Time and Resurrection* (Edinburgh: T. & T. Clark, 1976 [pb. 1998]).

1

ago.[2] It underlined the need for a theological and, as we shall argue as well, phenomenological and liturgical-sacramental consideration of the biblical data and this article of the Creed: "He ascended into heaven and is seated at the right hand of the Father."

1. A Question of Relevance

On the other hand, it might be thought that the ascension of Christ is so obvious as not to provoke much questioning. After all, the ascension and exaltation of Christ are the horizon in which the whole New Testament is set (John 20:17; Mark 16:19; Eph 4:8-10; 1 Tim 3:16; Heb 4:14; 9:27). Within that horizon, there is a continuing dialectic of Christ's presence and his absence, of what is past and what is to come, of the earthly time of Jesus and his resurrection from the tomb and the time of the Spirit, of sacramental realization and eschatological fulfillment. For Christian faith, time and space are redefined by the ascension: time now is no longer an empty succession of temporal moments or of ever inconclusive eras and epochs. Time unfolding under the gaze of the ascended One is fraught with the expectation and even longing for his return. It is moving toward a climax envisaged by faith and hope as the return in glory of the crucified, risen, and ascended Jesus. Something similar is to be said about space. Again, the ascension has caused a reshaping of our notions of place and space. As bodily beings, we live in place. But that place is set against a horizon unfolding into the indeterminable space of the world.[3] The Word incarnate shared an inevitable location. It meant living in a determined place in the world—the necessary restriction of being "here" rather than "there"—with all its experience of absence, distance, and marginalization. But his ascension has opened a new realm of space and location, cryptically described as his being taken up into heaven and taking his seat at the right hand of the Father. We shall have plenty of occasion to reflect further on such and similar phrases. Even though figurative language is inescapable, there is one

---

[2] Gerhard Lohfink, *Die Himmelfahrt Jesu: Untersuchungen zu die Himmelfahrts-und Erhohungstexten bei Lukas*, Studien zum Alten und Neuen Testament 26 (Munich: Kösel-Verlag, 1971).

[3] See Jean-Yves Lacoste, *Experience and the Absolute: Disputed Questions on the Humanity of Man*, trans. Mark Raftery-Skehan (New York: Fordham University Press, 2004), 8–10; 36–39.

thing that is clear. The ascended Jesus has not disappeared or been dissolved in a celestial ether, but is ever present to the faith of the church in the here-and-now of the community's life. The ending of his particular kind of terrestrial presence has yielded to a new kind of universal presence, reaching to all places, times, and peoples. His Spirit is poured out on all creation, the Eucharist is daily celebrated throughout the world, and Christians profess their faith in the words of the Creed, "He ascended into heaven and is seated at the right hand of the Father. He will come again in glory . . . ."

Far from being a largely irrelevant item in terms of Christian experience, the ascension is that facet of the Christian mystery that is most near to those living the life of faith. St. Paul, in emphasizing his relationship to Christ in the present, declared, "even though we once knew Christ from a human point of view, we know him no longer in that way" (2 Cor 5:16). Like him, believers of every age have no need to hanker after the earthly presence of Jesus in the Palestine of two thousand years ago. He has gone. He is risen, and has been exalted and glorified, and is Lord of all time and space. There is no point in gazing upward, as the heavenly messengers remind both the apostles and the generations who would profit from their witness (Acts 1:11). Faith and hope have now to be busy about other matters, even as Christians, then and now, await his return at the end of time, and the coming of the Holy Spirit (Acts 1:5, 11).

2. Resurrection and Ascension?

One might feel that everything has been said and implied in the resurrection event—even if the theological lack of attention to the resurrection of the crucified is itself often a matter of lamentation.[4] Besides, if theology has—heroically in some cases—insisted on the singularity of the resurrection of Jesus, it may feel it has exhausted its credibility by speaking of the ascension as further dimension. That extra consideration appears to introduce patently mythic elements,

---

[4] See Anthony J. Kelly, *The Resurrection Effect: Transforming Christian Life and Thought* (Maryknoll, NY: Orbis Books, 2008), 1–7. In this context, the works of Gerald O'Collins, SJ, stand out as remarkable incitements and resources for a richer theology of the resurrection. See his most recent work, *Believing in the Resurrection: the Meaning and Promise of the Risen Jesus* (Mahwah, NJ: Paulist Press, 2012).

or, at best, "apocalyptic props" of some kind.[5] Even when, quite rightly, the ascension is seen as an aspect of the early disciples' experience of the resurrection of the crucified Jesus, we must be careful of thinking, or giving the impression of thinking, that we know fully what the resurrection means and that the ascension is extrinsic or irrelevant to such meaning. It is not unusual that biblical references to the ascension are taken to be merely a coda at the end of the gospel, there to remain, and leaving faith none the wiser. Admittedly, the ascension is a liturgical feast of the church, esteemed by some as the high point of the liturgical year. Today, however, there is a peculiar modern confusion of celebrating it in many places on the Sunday instead of the traditional Thursday, as the glow of Paschaltide yields to the happy anticipation of Pentecost.

But the realism of faith intrudes. If Christians are to encounter Christ in the present, it is as the One who has been taken up into the mystery of God from which he came—however that is to be understood. Faith contacts him as having been glorified by the Father, having fully entered the divine realm of existence, vitality, and power when compared to his earthly state. Hence the Creed confesses him to be seated at the right hand of the Father, at the very throne of God. In his return to the Father, the Son shares the glory of God, acts with God's transforming power, and is present in the way that God is accessible.

And so, with regard to the ascension, something can and must be said—at least in terms of what is implied in that transformation in consciousness which Christians call "faith." In the words of Peter,

> Baptism . . . now saves you . . . as an appeal to God for a good conscience, through the resurrection of Jesus Christ, who has gone into heaven and is at the right hand of God, with angels, authorities, and powers made subject to him. (1 Pet 3:21-22)

If Christ "has gone into heaven," what does this mean for his presence to the church on earth? What has changed, what is promised, and what difference does it make to the life of faith? These are big questions and, to some extent, embarrassing as well. Still, it is

---

[5] J. A. Fitzmyer, "The Ascension of Christ and Pentecost," *Theological Studies* 45 (1984): 409–40.

not unusual for theology to be goaded into new creativity when it suffers its greatest embarrassment. There is a notable awkwardness for Christianity occasioned by the ostensibly outlandish claims so flagrantly contradicting the deeply set cultural mentality. In this case, faith has to contend with the late Western style of a deracinated rationalism. Even more to the point, there is the strange shadow side of the rationalist mindset, not only its antipathy to religious faith, but its crass literalism and inability to think figuratively in terms of symbols, metaphors, and multileveled modes of expression.

Christians, for the most part, have little trouble admitting that they do not understand Jesus as having gone up into the stratosphere after the manner of any number of gravity-defying objects such as balloons or rockets. In fact, in the present condition of faith, Christians have to admit that they see nothing of Christ with bodily eyes, and in the best biblical tradition see no point in scanning the sky for evidence of his going or return (Acts 1:11). The blessing of Jesus at the end of John's gospel is to the point: "Blessed are those who have not seen and yet have come to believe" (John 20:29). In short, in the language of faith, Jesus is not an object of sight—unless a particular visibility is taken into account, namely, that which occurs through the mediation of sacramental symbols, biblical images, icons, and religious art. Admittedly, there can be some special self-revelation of the otherwise invisible Christ, and a kind of seeing that finds God or Christ in the neighbor (Matt 25 and 1 John 4:20). On the other hand, faith implies a sense of personal intimacy with Christ, despite his invisibility. The words of the First Letter of Peter, in this respect, are especially striking:

> Although you have not seen him, you love him; and even though you do not see him now, you believe in him, and rejoice with an indescribable and glorious joy, for you are receiving the outcome of your faith, the salvation of your souls. (1 Pet 1:8-9)

The interplay of union with Christ and his invisibility implied in these words is bound to provoke questions in regard to the ascension. It is clearly a rupture—indeed a rupture twice over. Something has ceased. He is no longer a visible, tangible presence as he once was in his earthly life. That mode of living presence ceased with his death and burial. But there is a further rupture: his tomb remains empty, and he appears as one transformed and raised from the dead in what is reported as a series of postresurrectional self-manifestations. But that privileged period is over, whether interpreted as the forty days before his ascension, or in regard to the series of disclosures referred to by Paul, ending with his own encounter with the risen One. In other words, there is no question of Jesus returning to this present form of life, just as his episodic self-disclosures after his resurrection have come to an end (1 Cor 15:1-5).

If something ends with the ascension, if there is with it a sense of completion and fulfillment, something also begins. Jesus ascends to the Father from whom he received his mission and takes his place at the Father's right hand. His mission is complete and yields to the mission of the Holy Spirit, "the promise of the Father" (Luke 24:49). And yet he assures his followers that he remains always with them, and that he will come again at the end of time. What then emerges is a new mode of presence characterizing the time of the church and the witness of the Holy Spirit in all times and places. Or as that great champion of the ascension, Augustine,[6] would put it (in eschatological, ecclesial, and moral terms):

> Just as he ascended into heaven without departing from us, so we, too, are already there with him although that which he promised us has not yet been accomplished in our body . . . Although he ascended into heaven, we are not separated from him. He who descended from heaven does not begrudge it to us; on the contrary, he proclaims it in a certain manner: "Be my members if you wish to ascend into heaven. . . ." The body will be easily lifted to the heights of heaven if the weight of our sins does not press down upon our spirit.[7]

3. Rethinking the Ascension

We come therefore to this particular study of the ascension. Even though brief, it expresses a certain ambition to give more telling expression to the whole mystery of Christ from its concluding point

---

[6] For a succinct overview, see Wilhelm Geerlings, "Ascensio Christi," *Augustinus Lexikon*, vol. 1 (Basel: Schwabe, 1986–1994), 475–79.

[7] *Saint Augustine: Sermons on the Liturgical Seasons*, trans. Sister Mary Sarah Muldowney, RSM (New York: Fathers of the Church Inc., 1959), sermon 263, pp. 393–94.

in the ascension. The terms of the Christian narrative, whether explicit or not, reach from Jesus' beginnings—his conception, birth, and early life—through his healing actions and proclamation of the kingdom, on to his condemnation, torture, and death, and then to the three days of his burial and his rising from the tomb. Then there occur his episodic self-manifestations, followed by a new phase of invisibility—his ascension and definitive departure from this world.

Clearly, in the various New Testament accounts and references, we are not dealing with flatly stated facts. For instance, in the imagination of faith, the ascension is the high point of Christ's mission—"mission accomplished," we might say. He has returned to the Father; and, at the same time, sends the Holy Spirit and promises his future return.

All this is obvious enough to the most basic Christian theology, as it elaborates the articles of the Creed. What more can be said? Theological ambition is brought back to earth through the sheer weight of routine repetition of what is commonly taken for granted. What remains to be said? Is there any point in harrowing the exhausted soil after successive harvests? Why is this study needed? There can be only one answer: there is a continuing need to refresh our sense of the distinctiveness of Christian reality.[8] Today, all would admit that it is imperative that Christian faith be in dialogue with other versions of reality, religious and otherwise. That communication, however, will not bear fruit if Christian faith has lost its own distinctive sense of the real and has become somewhat stale, timid, and fuzzy in appearance. To counteract such a dismal possibility, and to strengthen the potential for dialogue, a theology of the ascension can inspire an open and inclusive understanding of Christian faith and the mission of the church.

How, then, is the ascension to be interpreted? What does it mean—for Jesus himself, for the church, for Christian faith? How is the ascension related to the resurrection of Jesus? How are both resurrection and ascension to be related to the incarnation itself? For example, does the ascension of Jesus mean that the incarnation—the Word become flesh—is somehow ended or made less real? How does

---

[8] See Anthony J. Kelly, CSsR, "Refreshing Experience: The Christ-Event as Fact, Classic, and Phenomenon," *Irish Theological Quarterly* 77, no. 4 (November 2012): 335–48.

the ascension affect our understanding of time, space, and bodily being? There are many questions.

If this study can throw light on some of these questions, it will be of value. To anticipate the general direction of our approach, we can suggest the overall vision connecting the various chapters in these terms.

4. A Preliminary Statement

What does the ascension mean both for Christ himself, and "for us and our salvation"? It may be useful to anticipate the fuller answer that will be given to these questions in the chapters to follow. But, as a preliminary statement, we can note that the ascension of Christ is a key event in the comprehensive sweep of the divine plan of salvation. The crucified Jesus rises from the tomb, and though transformed, appears to his disciples and is identified by them as the one who lived among them. He is then taken up into the luminous cloud of God's presence, no longer to be found in the time and space of his earthly life in Palestine, nor any longer revealing himself through the episodic appearances that followed his resurrection. In his ascended existence, he now fills all time and space, and inhabits every dimension of reality, from the highest realm of the infinite Godhead to the mundane, agonizing reality of created existence. The ascension opens the space in which believers themselves begin to inhabit a new sphere of transformed existence. God has "made us alive together with Christ . . . and raised us up with him, and seated us with him in the heavenly places" (Eph 2:4-6). The ascension is not simply the end of the journey for himself alone. It is of universal significance—a new beginning for all who will follow him since he embodies the destiny to which all are called.

In Jesus' passing from this world to the Father, there is certainly an ending of his earthly mission and an experience of his absence compared to his previous manner of presence. But the consciousness of faith registers a new mode of presence: "Behold, I am with you all days . . ." (Matt 28:20). Faith, therefore, does not cling to Jesus as a localized cult object. By letting him go into the glory of the Father, the faithful receive him back, in every moment and place, in the celebration of the Eucharist and through the gift of the Spirit. As faith follows him ascending into the glory of the Father, it is lifted beyond the world of projections, beyond the fantasy of gazing into an imaginary heaven for a lost hero. The focus of faith is, rather, always on the crucified and risen Jesus, as the One who has come and will keep on coming from out of the luminous reality of God into the reality of this world. As the white-robed heavenly interpreters told the "men of Galilee," "This Jesus, who has been taken up from you into heaven, will come in the same way as you saw him go into heaven (Acts 1:9-11).

The implication is that these natives of Galilee must now live as citizens of a much larger world. The whole of creation is filled with Christ's saving presence. From the glory of heaven, Christ fills the space left by his earthly absence. He has opened our world to the hitherto impenetrable reality of heaven, as he had promised his disciples, "you will see heaven opened and the angels of God ascending and descending on the Son of Man" (John 1:51). Jesus will be the new Jacob's ladder (Gen 28:12-17), connecting what is above with what is below. He is, in his person, the channel of communication between God and the world, so that his ascension opens up a God-given space for the unfolding of the whole history as it moves to its fulfillment. Because Christ has not shaken off the flesh of his humanity, human existence is already transfigured in him. The universe, and ourselves within it, has been drawn into the realm of God.

The ascension, therefore, manifests the boundless space in which Christ's victory over death and sin will be worked out. He is now "out of this world" in the sense that his absence, presence, and return are defined only by the infinite creativity of the Spirit—the divine cloud that received him out of sight. The ascension means, therefore, that in rising from the dead, Jesus is not reinserted into the fabric of the world that crucified him, subject to its desires, expectations, plans, and control. He is not resuscitated, but neither is he a kind of spiritual inspiration in a world unchanged and unchangeable. He has not ascended into the empty spaces that the world's calculations have left open, but "to the Father," to that realm in which the Father's will is accomplished, and the kingdom of God is already realized. He lives and communicates with the world of faith from the hitherto unattainable and still uncontrollable "beyond" of God.

5. Method, Focus—and Hope

So much for a general statement. Apart from helping to clarify what is an essential article of the Creed, there are other benefits to be had by meditating on the ascension. First, in the course of our investigation there will be a special benefit in terms of the method and focus, as we avail ourselves of some recent developments in phenomenology in order to keep the basic, original perception of Christ in the forefront of theological attention. That can counter the temptation to jump prematurely into abstract considerations that have become detached from the original experience of faith. It can happen that theology can be so defensively intent on the formulations of Christian doctrine that the original purpose and setting of such precise formulations are all but overlooked. The same might be said about a purely biblical-textual study which does not sufficiently focus on the experience of faith in the past, the present, and in every age of the church. I hope, therefore, to bring a phenomenological emphasis to this project, together with an attentiveness to the data in a way designed to respect the freshness of faith's experience of the reality of Christ.

Second, I will be attempting to emphasise the full reality of the incarnation. This will be presented as an expanding event of divine self-communication, so as to include the life, death, resurrection, and ascension of Christ and the ecclesial Spirit-formed reality of his Body. The mysteries of Christ are always interconnected in the one saving design of God. On the other hand, the incarnation is an expanding event as the Body of Christ grows throughout time. From that point of view, it is not that the risen and ascended Christ is no longer fully embodied but that we, his disciples, members, and followers, are not yet fully embodied in him within a transformed universe. In this context, as we shall see, the "body language" of the New Testament is instructive—and even tantalizing in its implications. An appreciation of the expanding reality of the incarnation in the light of the ascension is essential to the many-sided effort of communicating the good news of Christ in the dialogical world of our day.

But big questions stir beneath every sentence of this present work. Still, with due humility before mysteries beyond human sight and sound and imagination, we might hope to indicate at least the direction in which answers may be sought, and suggest the framework in which they might find expression in the future. In the ascension of the Lord, theology touches on an upper limit at which it is wisely silent for the most part. The ascended Christ, carrying our humanity with and in him into the realm of God, is not subject to the categories of the world from which he has departed. He now occupies a certain gravity-defying realm compared to our usual sense of proportion. Our thoughts and feelings are inevitably anchored in the world of routine experience, and so, are reluctant to go further. But faith follows Christ into glory and shares his joy as he ascends from the passion of the Cross and the terrible finality of death and burial to his present position as the right hand of the Father.

We must ask, therefore, "Is the contrast just too much, between his present state and our mortal humanity and the groaning of creation (Rom 8:19-25)?" So great is the Christian sense of solidarity with suffering others—oppressed by disease, deprivations, political and economic powers, and the systems that cause and support such miseries—that a celebration of the ascension cannot but appear as a fantastic distraction from the present world of grief. Are the glory and joy of the ascended Lord irrelevant to those committed to the struggle for freedom and flourishing in this present sphere? Dare a realistic faith follow him in his victory over death and in his return to the Father to celebrate the glory that was his before the foundation of the world? In a world of unfinished business, this side of the *eschaton*, can faith rejoice in his joy of completing the work that was his God-given mission?

I think that faith can find an essential and sober joy in that direction. It can and should, for faith needs to recover its radical joy. Without that, believers can be overwhelmed by the world of suffering—innocent or self-inflicted—that daily occupies our attention and shapes our sense of life as it is lived on this planet. Christ has come, and is now gone before us in order to find the joy and glory of divine life—for himself and "for us and our salvation"—the joy of love consummated, of life transformed, and of evil radically vanquished. Christian sensibility appreciates that the ascension is an entry into the realm of joy (cf. Luke 24:50)—the joy that the world can neither give nor take away.

Such radical joy does not entail a repression of suffering and sorrow. It does, however, found the conviction that in the risen and ascended Christ, all sorrow can be met, named, and even suffered, in hope and patience. One might suspect that a neglect of the resurrection—and its outcome in the ascension as the zone of joy and the realm from which the Spirit comes—has resulted in a certain depressive grimness in theology and perhaps even in Christian life. We cannot, and even dare not, speak too much of joy. But Jesus is not forever transfixed in agony on the cross, for he is now the living

One: "Do not be afraid; I am the first and the last, and the living one. I was dead, and see, I am alive forever; and I have the keys of death and of Hades" (Rev 1:17-18). He is the center of a new creation in which violence and death no longer rule, and are fated to be overcome entirely. From that perspective, the ascended Christ occupies a space and even a time—implying an absence and immeasurability compared to the time-space configurations of the empirical world. The space and time of the ascension are now relative to Christ in glory, the source of life and communion with the Father in the Spirit. Though Christ is, empirically speaking, absent to us, we are not absent to him. Indeed, his present absence has a purpose: that faith open itself to his new mode of universal presence and to the time of salvation determined by his promised return.

A devotional Christian imagination and various forms of meditation tend to focus on the particular conditions of time, place, and personal association as found in the gospels. But such practices are at their most healthy when they are set within the horizon opening up from the resurrection and ascension of Christ. When the paschal mystery is understood and celebrated in its full narrative extent, the words of Jesus addressed to the Samaritan woman in the Gospel of John are particularly relevant: "the hour is coming, when true worshipers will worship the Father neither on this mountain nor in Jerusalem" (John 4:21). In the hour of salvation, "true worshipers will worship the Father in spirit and truth" (John 4:23). In this new era, true worshipers would not be confined to "this mountain or Jerusalem"—or to Melbourne, Paris, Rome, Washington, or Delhi. To adore the real God is to live within the horizon of the Father's love for the whole world. In other words, Christ, by being absent from the fixities of time and place that once structured his earthly life, has ascended into the divine realm of presence and action. A new realm of relationship to the Father is opening up; heaven itself has been opened (cf. John 1:51). The space and time of salvation englobe all places, divisions, and separations. All the particular and general categories by which the limited world is constructed and times of its history assessed are transcended. In short, by ascending and now sitting at the right hand of the Father, Christ occupies all time and space, the totality of the God-ordered world as it is loved by the Father in sending his Son, and as subject to the Spirit's saving action.

In this present era of interreligious dialogue, belief in the ascension is of great importance. This "departure" of Jesus from this world and the consequent expansion of the Christ Event beyond the dimensions of the earthly life of Jesus of Nazareth serves to arrest the distortions and "idolic" propensities of religious projections and allow for revelatory disclosure or epiphany by which the light of another world breaks through. If "in him all the fullness of God was pleased to dwell" (Col 1:19), the mystery of God is not simply *there* as our possession or under the control of faith. Rather, since Christ is demonstrably absent, he calls forth the ecstatic character of faith and the dispossession of the self that are conditions for entry into the kingdom of the Father.

6. An Incarnational Perspective

This present study aims to deepen and extend my previous work on the resurrection.[9] In that respect, I recognize the danger of veering, however unwittingly, in the direction of four possible distortions. These all result both from treating the incarnation, the resurrection, and the ascension in a too isolated and exclusive manner, and from losing a sense of the relationship between the ascension and the church. The first distortion results from being so intensely focused on the classic doctrine of the incarnation as to reduce the resurrection and the ascension of Christ to being only a proof or manifestation of the basic reality of the Word made flesh. However, only by understanding the incarnation as an event expanding, as it were, into the resurrection and the ascension, can a sound Christology be developed. After all, Jesus is not less human after rising from the dead, nor does he shed his humanity by ascending to the Father's right hand. Clearly, the resurrection and the ascension are dimensions of the one incarnational event, just as they express the hope that humanity finds in the transformed humanity of the risen and ascended Jesus. And so, in the effort to redress any imbalance in the presentation of the saving mystery of Christ, the resurrection and the ascension must be brought into clearer focus as dimensions of the incarnation itself.

But this brings us to a second type of distortion, namely, that of the resurrection of the crucified One occupying center stage in the emergence of Christian faith, to the exclusion of the ascension and even the incarnation. We cannot, of course, minimize the crucial importance of the resurrection. Indeed, the incarnation would never

[9] Anthony J. Kelly, *The Resurrection Effect: Transforming Christian Life and Thought* (Maryknoll, NY: Orbis Books, 2008).

have been confessed if Jesus had not risen from the dead. Clearly, too, there is a consistent New Testament emphasis on the resurrection as the foundational event from Christian faith. Nonetheless, despite such an emphasis on the resurrection, the significance of the ascension can be minimized. It can appear as merely a psychological resonance in the consciousness of believers, and, therefore, as simply a way of speaking about the all-important fact of the resurrection— with no inherent Christological significance. And so we pass on to the third type of distortion.

More rarely—at least for theology—there is the temptation to consider the ascension as so focused on the exaltation of Christ and his divine vindication that the resurrection as a specific event loses its historical edge. Consequently, the empty tomb, along with the appearances of the risen One in the period after the resurrection, have a literary significance at best, designed to serve faith's conviction of Jesus' vindication and exaltation.

Given the danger of such distortions, the only course for theology is to keep the four articles of the Creed in play, dealing respectively with the Word made flesh, his resurrection from the dead, his ascension to the Father's right hand, and the promise of his return. If the incarnational framework is dismantled, the notion of God's self-communication in Christ and the Spirit is quickly lost. If, at the other extreme, the ascension swallows up the distinctiveness of the resurrection, the realism of salvation in Christ is undermined, and his victory over sin and death reduced to an abstract mythological significance. If, however, the ascension drops out of the picture, not only is a considerable range of New Testament references set aside, but eschatological, cosmic, sacramental, and pneumatological dimensions of salvation in Christ are overlooked.

Then there is a fourth possibility of distortion, perhaps the most serious of all. It arises from the impression that the meaning of the ascension is to be found not in Jesus' ascent into heaven, but in his "ascending" into the church. The sorry outcome of this distorted view is that it leaves no room for the reality of the ascension within the unfolding of the paschal mystery itself as the focal event for Christian faith, and dissipates the possibility of any such understanding. In effect, by identifying the reality of the church with the ascended Jesus, the impression is given that the church contains him on its level and in its structures, words, and sacraments. The church therefore must allow for the real *absence* of Christ in the glory of the Father—even while at the same time celebrating his Real Presence.[10] While Jesus has completed his journey and returned to the Father, the church continues on its pilgrim path. In his ascended state, he is the *head*—not a "member"—of his Body, the church. In that capacity, he breathes his enlivening Spirit into his ecclesial Body and nourishes it with his eucharistic gift.

The various chapters of this volume are designed to correct any such false impressions. More positively, their aim is to respect each aspect of the divine economy of salvation. In my previous book, *The Resurrection Effect*, I emphasized the centrality of the resurrection, but with insufficient attention to the ascension. The desire to remedy that inattention led eventually to this book. Despite efforts to redress a long neglect of the resurrection in theology, the full significance of the resurrection of the crucified One cannot be appreciated without recognizing that other dimension—his ascent to the right hand of the Father and his consequent cosmic presence. In other words, the full meaning of the resurrection is accessible only in the ascension. But the ascension is essentially included in the action of the Father raising Jesus from the depths of death and condemnation. Too frequently, both resurrection and ascension are in danger of being underplayed, with little thought given to their interrelationship. Though there is always the irreplaceable centrality of the resurrection for Christian faith, its completion in the ascension demands consideration.

In what follows, we will be treating of the ascension not merely as a quasi-terminal event in the narrative unfolding of the life and mission of Jesus, but also as a necessary dimension of Christ's relationship to the Father and to his presence in the life of the church itself. For the contemplative imagination of faith, to be freshly receptive to God's action in Christ is to be taken from the empty tomb to the fullness of his presence at the right hand of the Father. There he is now to be found, above all creation, above all time and space—and identified by the name "above every name" (Phil 2:9).

7. The Chapters Ahead

Finally, a brief note on the content of the various chapters making up this book and filling out the meaning of its title, *Upward: Faith,*

---

[10] This is the whole point of Farrow's *Ascension and Ecclesia*.

Church, and the Ascension of Christ. By beginning with the relationship of the ascension of Christ with reference to faith and the church, we attempt to communicate that the mystery of Christ's ascension deeply affects the experience of faith and the life of the church, both objectively and subjectively: objectively, in that our comprehension of the Christian mystery is truncated and even distorted if the backdrop of the ascension is downplayed or bypassed. Subjectively, there are consequences. The believer is drawn into a sense of the distinctive reality of what has been revealed in Christ. He or she grows in hope as the dimensions of revelation unfold, and is invited to the practice of ecclesial faith, above all in the experience of the strange compatibility of the Real Presence in the Eucharist with the real absence of the ascended Christ. We speak of the "forgotten dimension" because there is so little written on the ascension. It is taken for granted in Christian life, to the detriment of faith's recognition of the "boundless riches of Christ" (Eph 3:8).

And so, chapter 1: "Jesus Ascends—Leaving a World of Questions" serves as an introduction to a whole range of questions posed by this article of the Creed and the difficulty of not lapsing into a mythological kind of understanding of it. To point the way ahead, we offered a brief statement of the meaning of the ascension as it holds together the chapters to follow.

Chapter 2: "The Ascension and the New Testament: A Multidimensional Impact," gives some indication of the variety of ways in which the ascension—or its equivalent—was experienced and understood, e.g., as an event, a movement, a state, a relocation, and an activity. Here, we can do little more than offer a schematic outline of a representative range of biblical data, while appealing to some notable biblical authorities in this area. What we wish to emphasise, however, is that the event of the ascension, however resistant to precise description and definition, had a multi-dimensional impact on the life and imagination of the church. It resonated in the lived experience of the earliest Christian communities in varied ways, and inspired the images, symbols, and narratives that shaped the horizon of New Testament faith and hope. Indeed, it is not so much a question of finding the ascension in the writings of the New Testament, but more a matter of interpreting those inspired writings in the light of the ascension as the exaltation and ever-present activity of Christ.

Chapter 3: "The Phenomenon of the Ascension: Recollecting the Experience," as the title implies, attempts to consider the ascension phenomenologically—"in the round," so to speak, to take into account its singularity and the historic, universal, and eschatological sweep of its significance. Such an effort constantly frustrates any theological system, and thereby points to the need of a more refined and flexible phenomenological perspective, grounding and shaping theological exploration, and even our reading of Scripture. Not only is any imposition of a perspective extrinsic to the biblical data to be avoided, but also something more immediate and inherent in the phenomenon is required: the event must be allowed to appear in its own right. Hence the need for a recollected attentiveness to what is being conveyed to the consciousness of faith through the words of Scripture and the biblical images in its receptivity to the presence of Christ, risen and ascended.

Chapter 4: "The Body of the Ascended Christ: The Expanding Incarnation" offers a more complex and sweeping idea of the ascension. It argues that, in the light of the ascension, the incarnation is not limited to the past alone, but is an expansive and inclusive event in the continuing economy of God's self-communication. Not only is Christ still incarnate, but we ourselves are already members of his paschal Body. This is more vital, more material, and specifically incarnational than a metaphorical "mystical body" of some kind. The consideration of the Body of Christ throws light on the Catholic doctrine of the Assumption of Mary, and, in turn, is enriched by it.

Chapter 5: "The Ascension and the Eucharist: Real Absence and Real Presence" considers the interrelationship between the ascension and the Eucharist. This relationship can be distorted if no connection is made between the Eucharist—and even the Real Presence—and the ascended Christ as a real absence. Neither the church nor the Eucharist "contains" Christ, for it is he who is the One who contains all things.

Chapter 6: "The Ascension: Out of Sight, and the Eyes of Faith" addresses the obvious fact that Jesus is no longer visible as he once was. And yet, it is clear in the life of faith that he is present in other ways. A question must be faced: How does this other manifold presence affect the consciousness of faith and its sense of his ascension? Is there any sense in which the ascended One reveals himself so as to become newly visible? Christ is risen and ascended, but not so as to be a visible object within the world. On the other hand, faith can see and sense the world and its history as taken up into the ascended Christ in eschatological anticipation of what is to come.

Chapter 7: "Theology in the Light of the Ascension" is both a summary and a synthesis. But it cannot but provoke further inquiry, and the manner in which past, present, and future are interrelated in the one divine economy. The narrative of the life, preaching, and death of Jesus are understandable only in the light of his resurrection and ascension. Unless backlit by such a radiance, there would be no story to tell and none worth the telling; and there would be no one in any age disposed to listen to it as a follower of Christ.

Chapter 8: "'Lift Up Your Hearts': Looking in the Right Direction" suggests that in this postmodern context, the *sursum corda* of the ascension invites faith to be bolder and more confident in its commitment to the distinctive character of Christian revelation and the sense of reality it communicates. The summons of *sursum corda* flowing from the ascension promotes a more creative catholicity, and allows more fully for the dimension of *sursum* or "upward"— that "other dimension" in the ecology of faith—whether we choose to name it in terms of transcendence, open-endedness, otherness, universality or mystery.

This summary preview having been offered, we pass on now to a consideration of the biblical data.

Chapter 2

The Ascension and the New Testament
A Multidimensional Impact

After the previous pages of introduction to the "world of questions" opened up by the ascension, we focus selectively on New Testament texts in preparation for a consideration of the theological and liturgical phenomenon of the ascension. Admittedly, we can do little more than offer a schematic outline of the rich range of biblical data, calling on expert biblical commentators in this area. What we wish to emphasise is that the event of the ascension, however resistant to precise description and definition, had a multidimensional impact on the life and imagination of the church. It resonated in the lived experience of the earliest Christian communities in varied ways, and inspired the images, symbols, and narratives that shaped the horizon of New Testament faith and hope. Without imposing a rigid grid on this variety, we can at least indicate some of the perspectives in which the ascension—or is equivalent—is viewed.

1. Preliminary Remarks

First and most clearly, we have the Lukan narrative linking the gospel to Acts with its explicit ending and promise. That particular narrative of Easter followed by the forty days is all but classical in any presentation of the ascension, even granting the differing contexts of Luke's presentation—for instance, the ending of the mission of Jesus in the gospel account, and the beginning of the mission of the church in the presentation of Acts.

Second, there are the more condensed Johannine and Pauline presentations of the Christ Event. These place a strong emphasis on the resurrection, even if this is compatible with a certain sense of incompletion in their respective accounts of the mission of Jesus, most notably in John 20:20.

Third, the description of the paschal event, with its narrative unfolding, moves in many different ways to speak of the state and activity of the risen and ascended One, now "seated at the Father's right hand"—or equivalent expressions. For example, by means of its temple symbolism, the Letter to the Hebrews depicts the intercessory role of Jesus now that he has pierced the veil, but without neglecting his cosmic status. In a different perspective, the Book of Revelation presents the now ascended and glorified One as the focus of all the powers of creation, and as one enjoying divine authority and status as "the lamb who was slain," now presiding over both history and the life of the church. Furthermore, it is always striking that in the great sweep of the cosmic Christologies, as found in the prologue of John and the Captivity Epistles, Christ's departure from this world occasions the discovery of the his protological and eschatological significance. Though he is no longer a determinate presence *in* the world, that world, now understood in its ultimate reality and direction, is contained *in* him. Any effort, benign or not, to locate Christ in the world of limitations, suffering, and rejection is now reversed. He is the all-inclusive salvific space, one might say—the whole is in him, and finds coherence and fulfillment in and through him. There is a distinct cosmic dimension to the ascension of the crucified and risen One and his sitting at the Father's right hand. What occurred in him calls for a reimagination of time and space, nature, and bodily existence itself.

Admittedly, it is no easy task when theology tries to do justice to the richness and diversity of the biblical witness to the resurrection and ascension. The difficulty is not lessened by the varieties of data and the contexts in which they occur; the problem is further compounded by the fact that, only in the light of Christ's conquest of sin and death revealed in his resurrection and ascension is the New Testament written. If faith is to be fully receptive to what has been given in its experience of revelation, it must continue to explore the meaning of this singular, world-transforming event—the resurrection, ascension, and exaltation of the crucified Jesus. Indeed, in this respect, the ascension is not simply a metaphorical ending to the historical reality of Jesus Christ, nor a symbolic expression of an elevated Christian consciousness, nor an empirical event bringing to a close other empirical events associated with the life and death of Jesus of Nazareth. Neither is it a projection born of disappointed hopes, for, as we shall see, it is a spur to the realism and defiant activity of a genuine eschatological hope—a hope against all hopes as evidenced in the witness of martyrs.

From whatever perspective, the ascension is a God-wrought and God-revealed event, frequently presented within a metaphoric movement of descent and ascent (cf. Rom 10: 6-7; Eph 1:20; 4:8-10; Col 2:12; Heb 4:14; 9:24; John 3:13; 6:62; 20:17; 1 Pet 3:22). It is saturated with everything that Jesus was and is and will be. It discloses a horizon in which his life, death, resurrection are presented in terms of their universal and cosmic significance, along with his embodiment in the church and presence in the sacraments of the liturgy. Only in such a horizon can the Christ Event be appreciated in its full salvific realism. The headship of the risen and ascended Lord over all creation is offered to faith and hope, not as the insertion of a mysterious reality and series of events into the fabric of the passing world, but as taking up that world and drawing it proleptically into the fullness of his eschatological reality. After these preliminary remarks, we move to indications of the meaning of the ascension drawn from the variety of New Testament data on this phenomenon.

2. Outline of New Testament Data

Luke-Acts[1]

The Lukan account of the transfiguration prepares for the explicit ascension narrative. The glorious vision of Jesus conversing with Moses and Elijah about "his departure [Gk: *exodon*], which he was about to accomplish in Jerusalem" foreshadow the eventual fulfillment of his existence and mission (Luke 9:29-36). As the narrative moves to the drama of the passion, the crucified Jesus is presented in another conversation, this time taking place between the two

---

[1] The point of reference here is Luke Timothy Johnson, *The Acts of the Apostles*, Sacra Pagina 5 (Collegeville, MN: Liturgical Press, 1992); A work that remains seminal is Gerhard Lohfink, *Die Himmelfahrt Jesu*, Studien zom Alten und Neuen Testament 26 (Munich: Kösel-Verlag, 1971). See especially 242–72.

criminals being crucified with him. One of the criminals requests, "Jesus, remember me when you come into your kingdom." Jesus replies, "Truly I tell you, today you will be with me in Paradise" (Luke 23:42-43). The future state of Jesus is one of solidarity with those who repent and believe in him: "you will be with me in Paradise."

What came to pass on the cross is retrospectively illuminated in the words of Jesus after his resurrection and subsequent "entry into his glory": "Was it not necessary that the Messiah should suffer these things and then enter into his glory?" (Luke 24:26). It is not exaggerated to see the whole of the gospel narrative as "ascensional." The hearts (Luke 24: 32) and minds (Luke 24:45) of the disciples are stirred by the presence of the risen One, leading them to the triumphant conclusion:

> Then he led them out as far as Bethany, and, lifting up his hands, he blessed them. While he was blessing them, he withdrew from them and was carried up into heaven. And they worshiped him, and returned to Jerusalem with great joy; and they were continually in the temple blessing God. (Luke 24:50-53)

It is noteworthy that the disciples' final vision of him whose arms had been stretched out on the cross is also the image of him with arms outstretched, but this time in blessing. He is removed from their sight and taken up to heaven while blessing them. As the source of blessings, he is the cause of joy, and is worshiped in the sacred space of the temple where the disciples persevere, blessing the God who has blessed them in Christ, the embodiment of all blessings. They allow Christ to leave them, and then turn to God in joy, without any hint of sadness. Clearly, his ascent does not bring desolation, but results in rejoicing appropriate to the fulfillment of his saving mission in the world.

Compared to the beginning of Acts, the time frame in Luke is notably condensed.[2] It appears to happen all in the one day, as the one event of his "departure" includes the resurrection, his appearances to the disciples, and his departure from them in the ascension. But as we move to Acts, it is immediately evident that the events of

---

[2] For a recent attempt to reinterpret the relationship between the ascension and the forty days, see Henk Jan de Yonge, "The Chronology of the Ascension Stories in Luke and Acts," *New Testament Studies* 59, no. 2 (April 2013): 151–71.

salvation are presented in a more spacious and extended manner—a distinctive Lukan periodization of the paschal event. The forty days "after his sufferings" are presented as a privileged time of meeting and conversing with the risen Lord about what he had been had most determined in life and mission, namely, "the kingdom of God" (Luke 4:43;6:20; 7:28; 9:2, 11,60, 62). The disciples are told to remain in Jerusalem and wait for another period of time, for "the promise of the Father," namely, the gift of the Spirit (Acts 1:1-5).

The conversation that follows has the disciples asking, "Is this the time when you will restore the kingdom to Israel?" (Acts 1:6). The pre-ascended Jesus introduces them into that time frame which is determined only by the will of the Father (Acts 1:7). While the disciples must remain in ignorance as to the timing of God's design, they, nonetheless, "will receive power when the Holy Spirit has come upon you" (Acts 1:8). Consequently, with the fulfillment of the promise of the Father, they receive the assurance, "you will be my witnesses in Jerusalem, in all Judaea and Samaria, and to the ends of the earth" (Acts 1:8). Their query regarding the restoration of "the kingdom to Israel" now fades into the boundlessly larger prospect of "the ends of the earth."

In this atmosphere of promise and prediction, the ascension of Jesus is described in quite restrained terms: "When he had said this, as they were watching, he was lifted up, and a cloud took him out of their sight" (Acts 1:9). The biblical symbolism of the "cloud" figures as a sign of the presence and activity of God (Exod 24:15-18; Luke 9:34; 21:27). The risen Jesus is thus depicted not as simply returning to earthly life, but as entering into a new realm, symbolized by the cloud of God's presence and his position at the Father's right hand.

The scene as depicted in Acts describes the disciples gazing upward, while two radiantly white-robed men address a question to them (Acts 1:11). This recalls a similar questioning of the women at the empty tomb: "Why do you look for the living among the dead?" (Luke 24:4-7). But this time it is not the women looking for the living among the dead, but of the apostles looking for the living Christ in their immediate world of time and space: "Men of Galilee, why do you stand looking up toward heaven? This Jesus who has been taken up from you into heaven" (Acts 1:11). Jesus exists now in another realm—and in another form of communication conditioned by the outpouring of his Spirit along with the promise of his return: "he will come in the same way as you saw him go into heaven" (Acts 1:11).

In the later, post-Pentecostal words of Peter, Jesus "exalted at the right hand of God, and having received from the Father the promise of the Holy Spirit, he has poured this out that you both see and hear" (Acts 2:32-34). Though the promise concerning the Holy Spirit has been kept, there is still a time of further waiting for the universal restoration, preceded by a time of repentance and forgiveness: "Jesus, who must remain in heaven until the time of universal restoration that God announced long ago through his holy prophets" (Acts 3:21; see also Acts 5:31-32)). Further, Stephen in the throes of his martyrdom, is filled with the Spirit and draws attention to his vision of the opened heaven, and Jesus ascended into glory: "But filled with the Holy Spirit, he gazed into heaven and saw the glory of God and Jesus standing at the right hand of God. 'Look,' he said, 'I see the heavens opened and the Son of Man standing at the right hand of God" (Acts 7:56).

The account of Stephen's death presumes that the risen and ascended Lord, though having irrevocably departed from this earthly life, is still vitally present and involved. Clearly, the paradigmatic instance of this is found in the narrative of Paul's call or conversion experience (Acts 9:1-19; see also Acts 22:1-21; 26:2-23). Saul is confronted by the risen Jesus, "Saul, Saul, why do you persecute me?" (9:4), who identifies himself, "I am Jesus whom you are persecuting" (9:5). In a more restrained fashion—despite its ecclesial importance—the Lord confronts Ananias to bring about a lesser kind of change of heart and perception, namely, that involved in accepting the former persecutor as Christ's "chosen instrument" (9:13-15), who will be shown "how much he must suffer for the sake of my name" (9:16).

Further, the respective encounters of Cornelius and Peter with the Lord and with one another (Acts 10:1-11:18), along with Philip's meeting with the Ethiopian court official (Acts 8:26-38), are events occurring within the time of the church. This time, after the ascension of Jesus and the coming of the Spirit, is the time for the breaking down of barriers for the realization and expansion of a new community.

Matthew and Mark

Needless to say, the there is nothing like the Lukan treatment of the ascension in the other Synoptics. In his Passion narrative, Matthew has Jesus addressing the high priest with the prediction, "from now on you will see the Son of Man seated at the right hand of Power and coming on the clouds of heaven" (Matt 26:64; see also Mark 14:62). Following the resurrection, the Eleven gather on a particular mountain in Galilee, and are commissioned to make disciples of all nations, and, through baptism, to gather them into the trinitarian communion of Father, Son, and Spirit. The emphasis is not on the ascension as the departure of Jesus from his disciples, but more of an "ascension" into a new mode of continuing presence and universal authority: "I am with you always, to the end of the age" (Matt 28:20). There is explicit mention, however, of the ascension in the longer ending of Mark. The "terror and amazement" of the fear-stricken women (Mark 16:8) now yield to a quite different experience on the part of Jesus' disciples:

> So then the Lord Jesus, after he had spoken to them, was taken up into heaven and sat down at the right hand of God. And they went out and proclaimed the good news everywhere, while the Lord worked with them and confirmed the message by the signs that accompanied it. (Mark 16:19-20)

Jesus is taken up into heaven and is seated at the right hand of God. The activity of the ascended Jesus continues: he works with his disciples and is the source of special signs of confirmation in the task of evangelization.

To summarize the Lukan and Synoptic perspectives, we might suggest that in Luke's presentation of the Christian narrative, the ascension is a clearly articulated event within a particular periodization. The gospel account of what seems to take place on the one day is extended in Acts to the forty days after the resurrection, followed by a further ten days waiting for the outpouring of the Spirit. In that regard, the ascension of Christ means that Jesus now exists in a field of communication and solidarity with the church in the present time of the Spirit. The dominant image is that of him blessing his disciples from on high, and empowering them for their mission and respective responsibilities (e.g., in the instances of Stephen, Paul, Ananias, Peter, Cornelius, and so on.) And yet there is a further time of waiting—for the return of Christ in order to fulfil what has irreversibly begun.

In Matthew, the emphasis is on the continuance of Jesus' empowering presence in the time of the church, and with no implication of his departure. The longer ending of Mark on the other hand allows both for the "relocation" of Jesus in the realm of God but together with his active involvement with his disciples on their evangelizing mission.

John[3]

The movement of "descent-ascent" structures John's presentation of the mission of Jesus and its fulfillment in his return to the Father and the glory that was his before the foundation of the world. In John, Jesus' descent and ascent are constitutive of his identity: "No one has ascended into heaven except the one who descended from heaven, the Son of Man" (John 3:13). Jesus' confrontation with his opposition makes him ask, "Does this offend you? Then what if you were to see the Son of Man ascending to where he was before?" (John 6:62). In that sense, of "seeing the Son of Man ascending," John's gospel can be understood as a prolonged witness to the ascension "in progress."

Certainly, Jesus' ascension to the Father means that he departs from the world of earthly life and communication. Yet there is no sense in which his ascent to the realm of glory is an isolated and individual privilege of no salvific consequence to others. His departure is not an act of abandonment, but a movement of positive significance for those he leaves behind:

> In my Father's house there are many dwelling places. If it were not so, would I have told you that I go to prepare a place for you? And if I go and prepare a place for you, I will come again and take you to myself, so that where I am, there you may be also. (John 14:2-4)

In the two-way path of the "opened heaven" (cf. John 1:51),[4] not only does Jesus go to prepare a place for his followers, but he will

---

[3] The principal point of reference here is Francis J. Moloney, *The Gospel of John*, Sacra Pagina 4 (Collegeville, MN: Liturgical Press, 1998). See also Anthony J. Kelly and Francis J. Moloney, *Experiencing God in the Gospel of John* (Mahwah, NJ: Paulist Press, 2003).

[4] Further comprehensive analysis of this "two way" movement and the meaning of "dwellings"—Jesus' going to the Father, and Jesus and the Father coming to dwell in and with believers—is found in J. McCaffrey, *The House with Many Rooms:*

also come again to gather them into his company within the spacious hospitality of his Father's house. His return to the Father enables him to accompany his disciples in their homecoming since he alone is "the way" (John 14:6). Admittedly, all spatial metaphors of going and returning await their fullest interpretation in the paschal mystery of his cross and resurrection. In fact, the glorified Jesus will himself become the new "house of my Father"—the new temple of God's dwelling with his people (cf. John 2:21—and the whole section, John 2:13-22).

John invites his readers into a deeply contemplative participation in Jesus' communication with the Father. The gospel is designed throughout to console and strengthen all who believe in the Son of God sent into the world on his saving mission. The prayer of Jesus first refers to the completion of his mission:

> I glorified you on earth by finishing the work you gave me to do. So now, Father, glorify me in your own presence with the glory I had in your presence before the world existed. (John 17:4-5)

This prayer of the Son does not envisage leaving the world without any communication from him. He is not leaving everyone and everything behind. His reunion with the Father in original glory continues to be a revelation to the world. Thus, his departure from the world, once his mission is complete, still intends to awaken that world to its original meaning as the object of God's self-giving love. Heaven opens out to enfold the world into that relationship that exceeds all created forms of belonging, namely, the communion existing between the Father and his Son and Word.

Jesus' departure from the world and his return to the Father has consequences for his disciples. They will dwell in the world in a new way. They are to be witnesses to what God is revealing: "And now I am no longer in the world, but they are in the world, and I am coming to you" (John 17:11). Jesus asks the Father "to protect them in your name that you have given me, so that they may be one as we are one" (John 17:11). His prayer opens to include all who will come

---

The Temple Theme of John 14:2-3 (Rome: Biblical Institute Press, 1988), and Mary Coloe, *God Dwells with Us: Temple Symbolism in the Fourth Gospel* (Collegeville, MN: Liturgical Press, 2001).

to faith through the witness of the disciples, through all times and in all places. In what his disciples have already become, and through what they will later do, a new community based in the unity the Father and the Son comes into being:

> I ask not only on behalf of these, but also on behalf of those who will believe in me through their word, that they may all be one. As you, Father, are in me, and I am in you, may they also be in us, so that the world may believe that you have sent me. (John 17: 20-21)

Significantly, the outreach of this community extends to the world that has hitherto been presented in ambiguous terms. In continuing the mission of the Son, the community of disciples gives witness to the intimate and unreserved character of God's love for the world. Though Jesus did not pray for the world as an abstract entity (John 17:9), the world as potentially open to the Father's gift has been presented, at times negatively, at times positively, as the sphere in which the design of the Father is to be realized. It is not being abandoned to the darkness, but summoned to the light—"that the world may believe":

> Father, I desire that those also, whom you have given me, may be with me where I am, to see my glory, which you have given me because you loved me before the foundation of the world. (John 17:24)

Jesus prays that the disciples given to him by the Father will be transported into a new sphere of existence, so as to be where he is. They are to receive the gift of a new vision—to behold his hitherto hidden glory (John 17:24a). In this new luminous horizon, their outlook will be determined not by the conditions and categories of the passing world, but by the Father's limitless original love for him. All history and the progress of events in the life of Jesus himself are held together in the Father's timeless love. Though the disciples will continue to experience the fractured and conflict-ridden existence of life in the world, there will be a dimension of wholeness, peace, and joy based on the assurance that the eternal project of the Father will be realized. Believers will be in the world, but not "of it," in their awareness of love in which the world was made, and of the life for which it is destined (John 17:11, 14-15, 16).

By leaving his disciples, Jesus has in effect relocated them. They live now in the divine realm of life and communion, and in the atmosphere of the Father's household of many dwellings (John 14:2-3). The followers of Jesus can anticipate a luminous consummation of their faith, with a hope founded in the desire and prayer of the "ascending" Jesus. In this prayer, they will accompany him, and indeed, are through him brought into the presence of the Father: "My Father and your Father, my God and your God" (John 20:17). He will continue to make the Father known (John 17:26a). The identity of the Son sent into the world can be understood only in terms of the Father's original love for him, and as overflowing for those identified with him: "that the love with which you have loved me may be in them, and I in them" (17:26b). Through their union with Jesus in his return to the Father, the disciples are drawn into a universe of mutual love and self-giving communion (John 13:34-35; 15:12, 17).

After the glory that has shone forth in the cross and resurrection, there can be no possibility of restricting Jesus to a previous world of relationships. He summons Mary Magdalene into the luminous darkness of a new relationship to him: "Do not hold on to me, because I have not yet ascended to the Father" (John 20:17a). In this new relationship to him, she had to take a message to the disciples, now named by Jesus "my brothers and sisters" (John 17:a): "I am ascending to my Father and your Father, to my God and your God." (John 20:17b). She is now to relate to him, not in terms of her past experience, but as to the One who has come from the Father and who is now returning to him. He is to be followed as "the way" to a new "Father-ward" relationship (John 14:6).

The "hour" of his glorification is not yet complete until its fruits appear, as believers are enfolded into the communion existing between the Father and the Son (John14:12, 28: 16:10, 28). In the arrival of this hour of glorification and Jesus' return to the Father, believers are empowered to invoke the Father of Jesus as "our Father," and his God as "our God." They are no longer disciples, nor even friends (John 15:15), but his "brothers and sisters" in the one communion of divine life: "that they may be one, even as we are one" (John 17:22).

In short, a spatial motif of descent-ascent is inscribed into the Gospel of John, in contrast to Luke's temporal periodization of the Christ Event. The ascent of Jesus to the Father throws light on the "opened heaven" he had previously promised (John 1:51). In his ascended state,

Jesus, though no longer in the world, remains turned toward his disciples, preparing a place for them, and above all, praying to the Father on their behalf. In that sense, the ascension is a sign of Jesus' perfect communion with the Father—even as this is shared with the disciples so that the world might believe. Not only is Jesus ascended, but also the disciples themselves are now in a profound sense "ascended" into the divine realm of the Father. The glorified Jesus transcends all worldly categories in this final phase of intimacy with the Father—and this he wills to share with his disciples.

Pauline Writings

Without entering into detailed questions concerning the authorship of what are known as the Captivity Epistles, we find in them a consistent and clear light thrown onto the status of the risen and glorified Christ. His present state is one of universal Lordship resulting from his exaltation. Paul's earlier Letter to the Corinthians is a clear indication of this conviction. As the New Adam, the risen One is "the first fruits of those who have died"—in anticipation of the destiny of all who, in a God-established order, will be made alive in him (1 Cor 15:20-21). The present activity of Christ is described as preparation for handing over "the kingdom to God the Father," pending the nullification of all resistance to the reign of God. But even now, Christ himself reigns, gradually subjecting every hostile and contrary force to himself—including death since "God has put all things in subjection under his feet" (1 Cor 15:26, citing Ps 8:6). The ultimate purpose is "that God may be all in all" (1 Cor 15:28). The time in which the exalted Christ reigns is conceived as a period of intense antagonistic activity, ending in his final surrender of everything to God.

Philippians provides eloquent testimony to Paul's desire to know "Christ and the power of his resurrection" (Phil 3:10) in response to the "heavenly call of God in Christ Jesus" (Phil 3:14). Conflict and struggle are inevitable for the hope that reaches forward to "completion by the day of Jesus Christ" (Phil 1:6, 10). The divisive forces of "selfish ambition or conceit" and of one's "own interests" (Phil 2:3-4) are to be countered by sharing in the mind of him who has been exalted above heaven and earth for "emptying himself" in obedience to the divine will for the glory of God, the Father. Being with Christ in the glory which he now possesses presupposes conformity to him in his surrender to God:

> Therefore God has highly exalted him, and gave him the
> name which is above every name, so that in the name of Jesus
> every knee should bend, in heaven, on earth and under the
> earth, and every tongue should confess that Jesus Christ is
> Lord to the glory of God the Father. (Phil 2:9-11)

God's conferral on Jesus of "the name above every name" is a
precious expression of the lived meaning of the ascension in Christian consciousness. The apostle's words communicate a vivid sense
of life opening out into new dimensions as a great transformation
takes effect. It is not only a question of Paul's individual destiny, but
the destiny of all to whom he preaches the Gospel, as they await the
full revelation of Christ:

> But our citizenship is in heaven, and it is from there that we
> are expecting a Savior, the Lord Jesus Christ. He will trans-
> form the body of our humiliation that it may be conformed
> to the body of his glory, by the power that also enables him
> to make all things subject to himself. (Phil 3:20-21)

The coming Lord Jesus Christ will act to transform this lowly and
limited form of existence into "the body of his glory," for in his transformed and exalted state he is already acting to transform creation
into his own image for the glory of God.

Ephesians makes clear that this present period of expectation and
hope promises its own transformation of mind and heart. Paul prays
that God will give the community a new intensity of illumination
and wisdom, that "you may know what is the hope to which he has
called you, what are the riches of his glorious inheritance among the
saints, and what is the immeasurable greatness of his power for us
who believe" (Eph 1:17-19).

The divine power at work is evidenced in the paradigmatic case
of the elevation of Christ, "when [God] raised him from the dead,
and seated him at his right hand in the heavenly places" (Eph 1:20).
The Christ whom God has so exalted is not only above all else in
the heavens, but all creation is also effectively subject to him as history unfolds. Christ is lifted up "far above all rule and authority and
power and dominion, and above every name that is named, not only
in this age, but also in the age to come. And he has put all things
under his feet . . ." (Eph 1:21-22). The grandeur of this cosmic and
eschatological vision comes down to earth, as it were, in that God

has wrought the resurrection and ascension of Christ, not to remove him from the human world, but to make him "head over all things for the church, which is his body, the fullness of him who fills all in all" (Eph 1:23). While this suggests an exalted view of the church, the church itself is not ascended, nor is it spared the tensions that Paul himself suffered, even though it is the fullness of Christ as his embodiment in a history of Spirit-powered witness.

Furthermore, Ephesians points to a transformation of consciousness brought about by God's grace and mercy. The result is a "new self, created according to the likeness of God" (Eph 4:24). This transformation takes the form of a great transition—from spiritual death to life, from the regions below to the heavenly places with Christ, from the vanity of the world to a share in the highest levels of honor—all as manifestations of the measureless prodigality of the grace of God:

> But God, who is rich in mercy, out of the great love with which he loved us even when we were dead through our trespasses, made us alive together with Christ—by grace you have been saved—and raised us up with him and seated us with him in the heavenly places in Christ Jesus, so that in the ages to come he might show the immeasurable riches of his grace in kindness towards us in Christ Jesus. (Eph 2:4-7)

The risen and ascended Christ is the source of gifts for the building up of the Body of Christ to its fullest dimensions. After his self-emptying descent in the lower parts of the earth, Christ ascends "above all heavens," not only that he might fill all things in a cosmic sense, but also that he might fill out the dimension of his Body with all the gifts necessary for its life, growth, and upbuilding in love:

> He who ascended is the same one who ascended far above all heavens, so that he might fill all things. The gifts he gave . . . to equip the saints for the work of ministry, for building up the body of Christ until all of us come to the unity of the faith and knowledge of the Son of God, to maturity, to the measure of the full stature of Christ. (Eph 4:10-13; see also the whole passage, Eph 4:7-16)

And yet the struggle goes on, taking on cosmic proportions. Union with the exalted Christ means confronting "the cosmic powers of this present darkness, against the spiritual forces of evil in the heavenly places" (Eph 6:11-12). In this context, Paul's words are a reminder that the ascended Body of Christ, Head and members, is not brought about by a mere effort of imagination![5]

In Colossians, the apostle prays that his readers will be strengthened by the Father who has raised Jesus from the dead. God has acted, and has "rescued us from the power of darkness and transferred us into the kingdom of his beloved Son, in whom we have redemption, the forgiveness of sins" (Col 1:11-14). By God's saving action, believers have been taken into that realm of the Son, characterized by present deliverance and forgiveness. This brings us to one of Paul's most evocative texts regarding the ascension of Christ and its effect on Christian consciousness. In many respects, it parallels the hymn cited in Philippians 2:9-11, and enlarges the sense of the psychological resonance of the ascension in Christian consciousness:

> So if you have been raised with Christ, seek the things that are above, where Christ is, seated as the right hand of God. Set your minds on things that are above, not on things that are on the earth, for you have died and your life is hidden with Christ in God. When Christ who is your life is revealed, then you will be revealed with him in glory. (Col 3:1-4)

The affective and moral horizon of Christian transformation is suggested. If, the apostle argues, his hearers are already sharing in the power of Christ's resurrection and in his ascended state, they must live in a state of conversion, taking them beyond mundane concerns and into a full appreciation of distinctive Christian reality. Christian identity is to be found on the other side of sharing in Christ's death, having "stripped off the old self . . . and having clothed yourself with the new self" (Col 3:9), just as the reality of life in Christ is hidden within the mystery of God until the moment of his self-revelation and glory.

Conclusion. Christ is risen and ascended as "the first fruits" of what God is bringing about. In this exalted state, the ascended one is "in action," transforming all creation and the minds, hearts, and even the body of believers. His exaltation follows from the abasement,

---

[5] Peter T. O'Brien, *The Letter to the Ephesians* (Grand Rapids, MI: Eerdmans, 1999), 467–68.

obedience, and self-emptying that must remain paradigmatic for Christian life as it inspires a recognition of Christ's Lordship in his power to transform all creation. Accordingly, the exaltation of the crucified One has cosmic effects—and involves Christians in a cosmic struggle against the powers of darkness. Indeed, the ascension and exaltation of Christ inspires a deeper level of engagement with the forces of evil.

Revelation[6]

In what appears to be a circular letter to seven churches in Asia Minor, the Book of Revelation presents the risen and exalted Christ with an astonishing prodigality of images and scenes, first of all addressing a number of early Christian communities in order to encourage them in their respective particular struggles. The Lamb who was slain now acts with plenipotentiary power, possessing no separate throne but as seated (or standing) on the throne of God (Rev 7:17; 22:1, 3). From the viewpoint of a remarkably high Christology, Jesus is closely associated with the One "who is and who was, and is to come" and with "the seven spirits who are before his throne," and is himself described as "the faithful witness, the firstborn from the dead, and the ruler of the kings of the earth" (Rev 1:4-5). In the seer's vision, Christ possesses all the splendor of creation and all the divine glory revealed in the history of Israel (Rev 1:12-16). He identifies himself, saying "I am the first and the last, and the living one. I was dead, and see, I am alive for evermore. And I have the keys of death and of Hades" (Rev 1:17).

Like God, Jesus is "the one who is to come." The reign of God and the Lamb leads not only to the New Jerusalem coming down from heaven, but to the return of Jesus himself: "See, I am coming soon" (Rev 22:7). The final prayer, "Come, Lord Jesus" (22:20) is inspired by the Spirit working in the church. It is uttered by those who attend to the message of Revelation, and all who are thirsting for the gift of eternal life:

---

[6] The point of reference here is Wilfrid J. Harrington, OP, *Revelation*, Sacra Pagina 16 (Collegeville, MN: Liturgical Press, 1993); Craig R. Koester, *Revelation and the End of All Things* (Grand Rapids, MI: Eerdmans, 2001); Richard Bauckham, *The Theology of the Book of Revelation* (Cambridge, UK: Cambridge University Press, 1993).

> The Spirit and the Bride say, "Come." And let everyone who
> hears say, "Come" And let everyone who is thirsty come. Let
> anyone who wishes take the water of life as a gift. (Rev 22:17)

The vision of the exaltation of the Lamb in heaven makes possible the interpretation of history as the time of the church. In faith,
patience, and expectation, it must await the return of Christ (Rev 1:8,
17; 21:6; 22:13), conscious of his place at the origin of God's creation (Rev 3:14; cf. 1 Cor 8:6; Col 1:15-17; Heb 1:2 and John 1:1-3).
God and Christ act in concert; and with God, Christ is presented as
always coming (Rev 2:5, 16; 3:11; 16:15; 22:6, 12, 20). The Lamb
who was slain belongs to the way God rules the world (Rev 5:6) and
brings about the salvation of the nations (Rev 15:3-4; 21:3). Whatever the plethora of images and dramatic scenes, what is clear is the
exaltation of Jesus in his sacrificial existence (Rev 19:13; see also
John 4:6-49). The cross is the mode in which God's salvific action
takes place, and the exemplar and inspiration of Christian life.

The divine rule of God and the Lamb leads to the heavenly Jerusalem, the bride of the Lamb (Rev 21:2, 9, 11-21; 22:14). There is
no localized temple, since the presence of God and the Lamb is unbounded (Rev 21:22). Just as space in the new heavenly realm cannot
confine the Lamb, time likewise is relativized to meet the proportions
of God's saving intention (Rev 1:11; 3: 22:10). From one point of view,
"The time is near!" (Rev 22:7, 12, 20); but in the patience of Christian
life, the question persists, "how long?" (Rev 6:10-11). Nonetheless,
the whole sweep of history must now be understood in the light of
Christ's victory over sin and death, and the divine patience manifested
in the outworking of God's salvific design. The world and the course
of history are to be judged from a heavenly perspective, in which our
human sense of time, space, and power are relativized. Such a perspective is mediated through the apocalyptic symbolism, consistently
raising the question of who is really the Lord of the world. In all this,
Christ is not absent, but intensely present and active in history and
in the church. He is precisely identified as Jesus, the Lamb who was
slain: "I was dead . . ." (Rev 1:17).

Conclusion. Jesus in his ascended and heavenly state possesses a
divine status and exercises lordship over all creation. The patience of
Christian hope looks forward both to Jesus returning, and also to the
heavenly city descending (Rev 21:9). The recognition of the present
exaltation of the Lamb inspires an eschatological interpretation

of history as the time of salvation. In this exalted and ascended state, Jesus is sovereignly active in a way leading to the glory of the unbounded presence of God and the Lamb in the heavenly Jerusalem.

Hebrews

The Letter to the Hebrews provides valuable data, especially in its vision of the activity of the risen and ascended Jesus.[7] Its author—and the first generation of its readers—presume the exaltation of Jesus, and what we might describe as his primordial and eschatological significance (see especially Heb 1:1-4). But the letter adds something more, namely, the activity of the ascended and glorified Jesus in heaven, described in terms of the high priestly Temple ritual. "These last days" (Heb 1:2) presuppose the Son's expiatory immersion in time and the resultant significance of his death and present exaltation. There is a frank acknowledgement of the gap between the ultimate design of God and our present experience of the world: "As it is, we do not yet see everything in subjection to them" (Heb 2:8). Nonetheless, Christ, risen, ascended, and exalted, bridges the gap for Christian faith: what is not in evidence for the human race as a whole has been strikingly clarified in the One we do "see":

> but we do see Jesus, who for a little time was made lower
> than the angels, now crowned with glory and honor because
> of the suffering of death, so that by the grace of God he might
> taste death for everyone. (Heb 2:9)

A great reversal has occurred: because of his abasement unto death, Christ has fulfilled his mission for the sake of all, freeing those "held in slavery by the fear of death" (Heb 2:15). As the Son, Jesus presides over the house of God, which is made up of those who hope in the divine promise (Heb 3:3-6). This hope must maintain its focus and confidence in the role of the exalted Christ as the great high priest:

> Since, then, we have a great high priest who has passed
> through the heavens, Jesus, the Son of God, let us hold fast
> to our confession. (Heb 4:14; see also Heb 7:26; 9:11-14)

---

[7] For further commentary and background, see Craig R. Koester, *Hebrews: A New Translation with Introduction and Commentary*, The Anchor Bible, vol. 36 (New York: Doubleday, 2001).

Hope is anchored in him, our forerunner, representative, and intercessor, for he has penetrated into the inner shrine of the sanctuary of God:

> We have this hope, a sure and steadfast anchor of the soul, a hope that enters the inner shrine behind the curtain, where Jesus, a forerunner on our behalf, has entered having become a high priest forever according to the order of Melchizedek. (Heb 6:19-20)

In his unique high-priestly capacity, Jesus acts as the mediator of salvation. His existence in heaven is one of solidarity for those who place their hope in him:

> He is able for all time to save those who approach God through him, since he always lives to make intercession for them. (Heb 7:25)

In God's design, not only is Jesus the Melchizedek-like high priestly intercessor. He also enjoys the uniqueness of exercising his ministry of salvation as one seated at the right hand of God:

> Now the main point in what we are saying is this: we have such a high priest, one who is seated at the right hand of the throne of the Majesty in the heavens, a minister in the sanctuary and the true tent that the Lord, and not any mortal has set up. (Heb 8:1-2)

In the presence of God, he continues in solidarity with "us" who must follow his way, "For Christ did not enter a sanctuary made by human hands, a mere copy of the true one, but he entered into heaven itself, now to appear in the presence of God on our behalf" (Heb 9:24). But he is not to be forever hidden from this world of ambiguities, for he will return as the bearer of salvation, and "will appear a second time, not to deal with sin, but to save those who are eagerly waiting for him" (Heb 9:27) and his ultimate victory over all opposition (Heb 10:12-13).

Jesus' exaltation as the "great priest over the house of God" opens for believers a "new and living way" into the mystery of God that is still shrouded from human sight. His ascension into heaven as our redeemer and intercessor means a spiritual ascension on the part of those who follow him, as the day of the Lord comes closer:

> Since we have confidence to enter the sanctuary by the blood
> of Jesus, by the new and living way when he opened for us
> through the curtain (that is, through his flesh) and since we
> have a great priest over the house of God, let us approach
> with a true heart in full assurance of faith . . . encouraging
> one another, and all the more as you see the Day approach-
> ing. (Heb 10:19-25)

The present heavenly status of Jesus presumes his transcendent
status, his primordial and eschatological significance and the salvific
efficacy of his death. As the unique high priest, Jesus has passed
through the veil, and now presides over the house of God. In his exalted state, he acts as forerunner, representative, and intercessor for
the faithful, exercising his role of mediator by being seated at God's
right hand. The divine plan of salvation will be achieved when Christ
appears a second time. But, in the meantime, his exaltation inspires
a spiritual ascension of faith and hope in those who follow him.

General Conclusion

A preliminary classification of this rich variety of data suggests
the following perspectives on the ascension of Christ:

1. a distinct event terminating the mission of Jesus—above all in
   the classic narrative of Luke-Acts
2. the quasi-ascent and departure to the Father (e.g., John 13:1;
   John 17, John 20:17)
3. exaltation by God: the Father glorifies the Son
4. a range of activities of Jesus at the right hand of the Father
   (e.g., sending the Spirit, subjecting all creation to himself for
   the glory of God, and being actively present to the church)
5. departure and absence for the sake of new mode of presence
   and final coming
6. the transformation of Christian consciousness: *sursum corda*
7. data concerning the ascension in the New Testament, but
   also the emergence of the New Testament in the light of the
   ascension

We are now in a position to deepen and refine our response to
this rich and diverse range of data by moving on to reflect on the
ascension as a phenomenon in the experience of Christian faith.

Chapter 3

The Phenomenon
of the Ascension
Recollecting the Experience

After our somewhat schematic selection of New Testament texts and perspectives, we move now to consider the ascension phenomenologically—"in the round," so to speak. That will mean taking into account the singularity of this event, and the historic, universal, and eschatological sweep of its significance. Such efforts constantly frustrate any theological system and thereby point to the need for a more refined and flexible phenomenological perspective, grounding and shaping theological exploration. Such an attitude tries to allow for a full play of interweaving considerations of the ascension as this particular salvific event (and article of the Creed), and yet hold it apart from the mundane phenomena of a gravity-defying type to which it is too often reduced.

Not only is any imposition of a perspective extrinsic to the biblical data to be avoided in this effort, but also something more immediate and inherent in the phenomenon is required: the event must be allowed to appear in its own right.[1] Hence the need for a recollected attentiveness to what is being conveyed to the consciousness of faith

---

[1] A phenomenological prelude to systematic exposition has the advantage of precluding a false opposition between the epistemological—that is, the resurrection and ascension simply manifest the transcendent character of the revealed Word—and the ontological—that is, these events are real in themselves and part of the objective unfolding of God's saving action. On this point, see Douglas Farrow, "Karl Barth on the Ascension: An Appreciation and Critique," *International Journal of Systematic Theology* 2, no. 2 (July 2000): 127–50.

through the words of Scripture and the biblical images in its receptivity to the presence of Christ, risen and ascended.

1. The Overarching Phenomenon

A theological phenomenology attends to various features of the ascension in the experience of faith such as an ending, a departure, an ascent to invisibility, exaltation, divine status, spiritual empowerment, and promise of the consummation of history. Each of such aspects bears out the meaning of Paul's words regarding, "the mystery that has been hidden throughout the ages and generations but has now been revealed to his saints . . . Christ in you, the hope of glory" (Col 1:26-27).

What is immediately evident is a convergence of perspectives in regard to what has occurred. The compact experience of the risen Christ (Paul, John) and the narrative of what took place occurring in different time-structured phases (Luke-Acts), the awareness of its cosmic dimensions (Revelation, Hebrews, Captivity Epistles) is presented to faith as a God-wrought decisive event. It is therefore of theological and salvific significance. The act of God's "raising" Jesus from the dead and then taking him up into heaven where he is glorified and enthroned, not only has consequences for Jesus, but also has an overflow effect on all who follow him—even to the point of their enjoying a spiritual ascension already (e.g., Col 3:1-4 and Aquinas *STh* III, q. 57, a. 6).

A basic feature of this act of God is that it brings to an end a certain economy of Jesus' visibility, whether in terms of the natural frame of Jesus' earthly life and violent death, or in regard to his self-disclosures after his death as the risen One. Yet the end is also a beginning of another phase of the divine economy. Though disappeared from historical view in terms of immediate presence, Jesus will move history onward from a divine vantage point with the power and enlightenment of the Spirit; and, in his return, will himself consummate that history as its redeemer and judge.

Theology must develop appropriate receptivity to the biblical accounts and depictions of the ascension in order to appreciate their experiential depth and salvific significance. But that does not entail leaving the event of ascension to the past as though it were an isolated happening in a Ptolemaic cosmos. Indeed, in terms of the cosmology of this much later time, it might well be that the ascension will have a more real and significant impact on the faithful than could have been the case for the early ages of the church. Be that as it may, the ascension as a Christian mystery continues to be powerfully mediated in the liturgy of Paschaltide. The life of the church unfolds within a horizon formed in its every dimension by a sequence of feasts and mysteries focused on him who was once amongst us in the flesh, who died and was buried, rose from the tomb, and is now taken up into the heaven of God—whence he will come again—as expressed in the lapidary articles of the Creed.

Yet theology might hesitate and try to cover its embarrassment. One might ignore the phenomenon of the ascension as beneath consideration because of its mythological resonances. Another might offer such thin theoretical account that it does little more than repeat the words of the Creed: "he ascended into heaven, and sits at the right hand of the Father." Whatever the case, there can be no question of embarking on a systematic and theoretic analysis of what the ascension of Christ means without first recovering a sense of what it is that is being explored and analyzed. Before faith seeks understanding, it must first absorb what has been given into, and received by, its consciousness. Such a receptive and disciplined openness must respect the terms and manner in which what has been given or revealed has in fact come into the awareness of faith. The phenomenon cannot be critically examined without registering the *phenomenality*—the manner in which it has been given—of its occurrence and appearance. Just how the event of the ascension impinges on the consciousness of faith is a question that inquires into the experience of the earliest disciples, and the manner in which it finds differing modes of expression in the biblical accounts and references in quite a variety of contexts—in, say, that narrative structure of Luke-Acts compared to the writings of John and Paul, and the particular perspectives represented in the Book of Revelation or the Letter to the Hebrews, as we indicated in the previous chapter.

The singular phenomenon of the ascension underlies the biblical and liturgical experience of faith. It indicates an event of both profound and pervasive theological significance. God has acted. Faith is taken to the limit of the "visible mission" of the Word made flesh. Jesus, crucified and risen, is taken up, "out of sight," into the realm of God's presence. He exists now as the exalted One, sharing in the divine glory and possessing power to act in all times and places.

But before considering the particular phenomenon of the ascension, a more general consideration will be useful. The various New Testament narrative and visionary expressions of the Christ Event, and of the ascension in particular, arise out of an alert receptivity to what has been given, and continues to be given, in the consciousness of Christian faith. What is routinely taken *for granted* in theological discourse as data for analysis and reflection requires a prior, deeper receptivity as to the manner in which it is revealed. What theology takes for granted must be first of all taken *as granted* in a particular way.[2] After all, the data of theology deal primarily with the grace, the gift of God, and God's self-communication. The data, in other words, are the "given," not only as impinging on human consciousness, but as originating in a divine initiative, as *dona* ("gifts").

2. The Theological Phenomenological Perspective

Philosophers have long stressed the need to cultivate an open, alert, and refined receptivity to all the phenomena occurring in human experience. A closed mind or a deliberately restricted horizon in regard to the possible does not promise well.[3] In contrast, a critical phenomenological approach calls into question the naïveté of situating everything within the narrow band of everyday experiences, and so suspends the habitual convictions about the "real world" that arise from such narrowness. Speaking generally, the aim must be to throw light on the manner in which meaning arises, be it philosophical, literary, or theological. That means trying to investigate the elemental experiences that provoke questions that need to be answered: What has happened? What is going on? What difference does it make?—and so forth. This counters the temptation to collapse everything into a monodimensional outlook, and prevents discussion being snagged on predetermined notions of the possible and the knowable. In other words, we must allow ourselves to be freshly "struck," as it were, by the sheer originality of what has oc-

---

[2] For the following remarks, I am especially indebted to Anthony J. Steinbock, *Phenomenology and Mysticism: The Verticality of Religious Experience* (Bloomington and Indianapolis: Indiana University Press, 2009), 1–27. More generally, I am grateful for the contribution of such writers as Kevin Hart, Jean-Luc Marion, Michel Henry, Claude Romano, and others, as is evident in my previous work, Anthony J. Kelly, *The Resurrection Effect: Transforming Christian Life and Thought* (Maryknoll, NY: Orbis Books, 2008). See especially 24–43.

[3] Max Scheler, *Vom Ewigen im Menschen*, Gessamelte Werke, vol. 5 (Bern: Franke), 250, cited in Steinbock, *Phenomenology and Mysticism*, 6.

curred and the way it is or was experienced. When the focus is on what is consciously experienced, reality begins to be experienced in its arresting and particular otherness.

In a theological perspective, the *data*—the given content of experience—derive from the *donum*—the gift that comes with a giving and from a giver beyond any worldly horizon. Mundane horizons of the possible, the real and the knowable, are interrupted by a vertical in-breaking of an event "not of this world." It is not surprising, therefore, that the religious or theological dimension is insignificant to mentalities enclosed in their own narrowness. What is lost is that other dimension—the vertical dimension of the height and depth of experience.[4] This exceeds a purely empirical appearance or narrowly rational analysis, thus disturbing the settled horizons of mundane understanding and calculation.[5] An irruption has occurred; and in a mode of givenness that is traditionally termed, "revelation" and "epiphany." Consequently, there is a vector of surprise and grace within the possibilities of human experience.[6] A gift is given from beyond all human giving, from a giver who is not of this world.

Receptivity to the gift presupposes the interpersonal experience of a community of faith and its animating tradition formed by sacred texts, doctrines, symbols, sacraments, and examples of holiness.[7] The Christ Event introduces a new horizon in which the transformative act of God's love affects every dimension of consciousness. It extends and reorders the scale of values and gives rise to new dimensions of meaning in our understanding of God, the self and the world. Settled horizons of expectation are upset and disrupted with the excess, both attractive and demanding, of God's self-giving in Christ. Whether unobtrusively or dramatically, consciousness is affected by the Christ Event so as to expand in new horizontal and vertical dimensions. As St Paul would put it, "for those who are in Christ, there is a new creation" (2 Cor 5:17). In its receptivity to the revelatory event, Christian theology is less thinking *about* some object or proposition of belief, and is more a form of thinking

[4] Steinbock, *Phenomenology and Mysticism*, 9.

[5] Ibid., 9–10.

[6] Ibid., 14.

[7] Edward Farley, *Ecclesial Man: A Social Phenomenology of Faith and Reality* (Philadelphia, PA: Fortress Press, 1975) is still a valuable exposition of the phenomenology of the corporate Christian reality.

from *within* the experience of what is given within the community of the faithful. The first act of reflective faith is to allow the Christ Event to appear in its arresting "otherness" and provocative power. In the receptivity of faith, the rational, all-critical ego no longer occupies center stage, as though "subjecting" everything to its powers of reason.[8] The believer, rather, is the one who is "subjected" to what is graciously and provocatively disclosed to him or her in the paschal mystery of Christ's death, resurrection, and ascension.[9] This revelatory experience inspires a distinctive tradition of rationality, morality, and art as its contribution to the world's history.[10] Human reason is not allowed to remain undisturbed in isolation from the reasons of the heart that reason cannot know. A difference enters into the creativity of human intelligence when it is affected by the love that "bears all things, hopes all things, endures all things" (1 Cor 13:7-8).

3. The Ascension as Singular Phenomenon

The ascension is indeed a multifaceted mystery of faith—an ending and a beginning, a fulfillment and a promise, a departure and a return, and much else besides. In a previous book on the resurrection,[11] I had occasion to refer to the many-sided phenomenon of the paschal mystery of Christ. To this end, I profited especially from the writings of Jean-Luc Marion, among others. It was clear that his analysis of a number of "saturated phenomena" could throw light on the experience of faith,[12] and the manner in which faith must mean receptivity to the divine gift.[13] Let us touch briefly on such phenomena, overbrimming as they do all routine boundaries and frames of reference.

---

[8] Jean-Luc Marion, *Being Given: Toward a Phenomenology of Givenness*, trans. Jeffrey L. Kossky (Stanford, CA: Stanford University Press, 2002), 261.

[9] See Kelly, *The Resurrection Effect*, 29–42.

[10] Neil Ormerod, *Meaning, Method and Revelation: The Meaning and Function of Revelation in Bernard Lonergan's* Method in Theology (Lanham, MD: University Press of America, 2000), 217–19.

[11] Kelly, *The Resurrection Effect*, 27–43.

[12] Marion, *Being Given*, 234–36.

[13] Ibid., 5.

The Ascension as Revelation[14]

The phenomenon of the ascension is situated within the larger phenomenology of Christian revelation. Post-Enlightenment philosophical difficulties are well known, given that there is an entrenched speculative conviction against the very possibility of divine revelation. In the meantime, Christian faith lives in a milieu determined by the self-revelation of God in Christ. Jesus is in person the phenomenon saturating the whole of the New Testament and Christian life. He is given in a way of excess in his death, resurrection, and ascension, overbrimming and disrupting all previous categories and expectations. The world of his previous relationships is radically rearranged: the Word becomes flesh, and in that flesh, he is crucified, and raised from the dead—and ascends into heaven. The inexhaustible excess presented to faith frustrates any human expression of the event, at once within the world and yet beyond it (see John 21:25). Receptivity to the phenomenon of Christ must allow it to appear in its own evidence and on its own terms. Accordingly, there is an inevitable interplay of giving and receptivity, of appearance and invisibility, of presence and absence, of the horizontal and the vertical. Yet this revelation continues to have a manifold effect in the life and mission of the church. Though the cloud receives the ascended One and renders him "out of sight," faith, even in this era of "not seeing" compared to the "seeing" of privileged post-resurrectional witnesses, is not a form of blindness, let alone a commitment to nothing and a relationship to no one. The risen and ascended One, although no longer a presence within the world in the way he once inhabited it, still inspires all the "senses" of faith. Faith tastes the goodness of God and listens to the Word.[15] It breathes the Holy Spirit and eats and drinks the sacramental realities of Christ's Body and Blood, just as it is strengthened by the foundational testimony of privileged "eye witnesses" and the cumulative evidence of transformed lives. Through all this, the self-revealing phenomenon of Christ draws believers into its field, and summons to a conversion that is never complete in this life.

[14] For the various instances of and reference to saturated phenomena such as revelation, event, esthetic form, face and body, see Kelly, *The Resurrection Effect*, 30–43.

[15] For a theological phenomenology of voice, see Sergio Gaburro, *La Voce della Rivelazione: Fenomenologia della Voce per una Teologia della Rivelazione* (Milano: Edizioni San Paolo, 2005).

From one perspective, the revelatory impact of the ascension is such that it is not one act of divine self-revelation among many, but the culminating act of God's self-revelation in Christ, and, in him, of the reconciliation of the world with God. As a God-wrought and God-revealing event, it catches up everything that Jesus was, and is, and will be to form the horizon in which his life, death, resurrection are disclosed in terms of their universal significance. Only against such a horizon can the Christ Event be appreciated in its full salvific realism. For the ascension is the overarching presupposition and backdrop to Christ's embodiment in the church and presence in the Eucharist. The Father's exaltation of crucified, risen, and ascended Lord over all creation occurs not as the insertion of mysterious reality into the fabric of the passing world, but as the taking up of that world into the fullness of his eschatological reality. Nonetheless, even supposing the influence of the ascension in determining the horizon in which the various aspects of the life and mission of Christ are integrated and related, we must stress that there is still an absence. While the ascension provides the horizon in which Christ is present to the community of faith, it is also the realm from which he must return—and in which, therefore, he is now absent. Such is the revelatory paradox of the ascension: Christ's ascent into the heaven of God means waiting on the time of God and hoping for what is beyond human calculation. If the ascension cannot be separated from the resurrection preceding it, it cannot be considered apart from the return of Christ in glory.

The Ascension as Event

The revelatory impact of the ascension cannot be separated from its occurrence as an event.[16] Something happened; and when something of great significance happens, it possesses a singular and expanding impact. Its meaning is not to be found in previous notions of the real or the possible, for the "excess" overflows any calculus of cause and effect. The origin and emergent influence of such a happening can never be fully grasped.[17] Great tragedies overflow the bounds of rationality,[18] just as, in a more positive vein, the historical

---

[16] Kelly, *The Resurrection Effect*, 32–33.
[17] Marion, *Being Given*, 140, 165, 172.
[18] Ibid., 201.

emergence of Christianity and its connection to the birth, life, death, and resurrection of Jesus of Nazareth is world shaping in its proportions. The attempts of cultural rationality to reduce such events to a circumscribable object cannot cope with the overwhelming character of what has taken place. When a truly revelatory event occurs beyond all previous calculations, it intimately involves those caught up in it. The world of one's previous life is reconfigured and made newly meaningful and significant. It inspires manifold change and radical conversion of mind, heart, and imagination through faith in Christ, many other forms of religious experience, or as a momentous breakthrough in the worlds of science, art, or law and government.

Momentous events give rise to a certain "anarchy," as the fixed points of previous horizons are dramatically shifted. The full significance of what has happened can emerge only with time and in patiently awaiting the future to unfold.[19] When such an event takes place, the only possible response is not one of projecting new possibilities onto an already rationally established world, but of becoming involved in a world made new and newly understood, outside any previous horizon.[20] Something new has been born.[21]

The ascension of the crucified and risen Jesus is a world-changing event. The death-bound horizon of human destiny now changes into an anticipation of a reconciled future of life with God in the communion of saints. In the risen and ascended One, our humanity is taken up to be with God, and the world itself is viewed in the light of him who is the firstborn of all creation and firstborn from the dead (Col 1:15-18). Such is the boundless and transforming power of this radical event, that Paul can write, "if anyone is in Christ, there is a new creation: everything old has passed away; see, everything has become new!" (2 Cor 5:17). The new life represented in him can be understood as a new birth and the beginning of an eschatological fulfillment (1 John 3:2). In the horizon illumined by Christ's ascension, the believer receives the assurance of being already carried toward the Father's house which Jesus now occupies. As he prepares a place for his followers he assures them, "I will come again and take you to myself, so that where I am, there you may be also (John 14:2-4).

---

[19] Claude Romano, *L'événement et le monde*. Épithée. Essais Philosophiques (Paris: Presses Universitaires de France, 1998), 60–69.

[20] Lacoste, *Experience and the Absolute*, 8–10, 37–39.

[21] Romano, *L'événement et le monde*, 72–96.

In the total phenomenon of the Christ Event, the events of the resurrection and the ascension can be distinguished in certain scriptural and theological contexts, even if they are not separable. The simplest and clearest way of expressing such inseparability is to suggest that the event of the resurrection has its ultimate effect and universal impact when located in the horizon opened up by the ascension. Christ has left the death-bound world behind, and, in his humanity, carried that world into the deathless realm of God and eternal life. While the Spirit is sent from the realm to which Christ has ascended, the church and its sacraments mediate in presence-in-absence. Time is newly begun and finds its focus on the endpoint of Christ's return as the consummation of history.

For its part, the effect of the ascension is to locate the event of the resurrection within its properly transcendent, universal, and cosmic horizon of significance. The resurrection without the ascension can easily be reduced to a particular past happening and be deprived of the universal salvific relevance proper to it. The ascension separated from the resurrection can be reduced merely to a "higher point of view" uncontaminated by any momentous historical experience of a singular event. In that case, it would not entail the ascent of our humanity in Christ to the Father with its already realized victory over sin and death. Were that the case, ascension would amount only to ideological abstraction, an ascent into a religious ether—not the ascension of the crucified and risen One to his universal and cosmic Lordship.

The Ascension as Aesthetic Form

The beautiful has a distinctive, attractive, and transforming effect. A work of art—for example, a great painting—in striking us with its beauty, frames the world in a new way, while overflowing the capacities of any particular perception of it. It cannot be merely a tasteful adornment to the décor of a room, for its aesthetic impact causes everything to be rearranged in the living space of our routine experience. It invites an endless contemplation in ways that go beyond the flat manner of looking at—or possessing—any ordinary object.[22] Those who are receptive, with their varying sensitivities and appreciative

---

[22] Marion, *Being Given*, 203.

capacities, enter into the world framed by the picture, and so see the world afresh. The artist does not so much depict an arresting object within the routine scope of cultural vision as disclose something or some dimension in the light of something other and something more.

The revelatory event of the ascended Christ is first of all a glory,[23] a beauty, and with its own attractive force: "And I, when I am lifted up, will draw all people to myself" (John 12:12). Christ crucified, risen, and ascended comes as a *Gestalt*, an irreducibly concrete, whole, and complete form. It is not only a matter of seeing this form, for it also invites participation in the whole of the Christian mystery.[24] The risen and ascended One transcends the world of expression and draws those who receive him into the world of the gift, into a universe of grace, into the excess of self-giving and to the original and ultimate Giver.[25]

The Ascension and the Body

Ascension does not mean "excarnation," but the expansion of the incarnation into the Body of Christ. We will treat the ascension in relation to the incarnation as an expanding event in a later chapter. In anticipation, we note how the phenomenon of the body or "the flesh," is not merely a material or biological entity, but the zone of interweaving, incarnated relationships.[26] Experience "in the flesh" affects and is affected by the larger phenomenon of the world. For the flesh, or embodied existence, is at once an original bonding with the world, an immediate exposure to it, an immediate participation in it, and a primal communication within it.

The ascension does not mean the dissolution of the incarnation. The Word became flesh; and in that flesh, he is crucified, raised from the dead, and ascended into heaven. The flesh, the Body of Christ with all its individuality is, even in this time of the ascension, God's

---

[23] Theology is indebted to Hans Urs von Balthasar, as in his *The Glory of the Lord: A Theological Aesthetics*, ed. Joseph Fessio and John Riches, trans. Erasmo Leiva-Merikakis, vol. 1: *Seeing the Form* (Edinburgh: T. & T. Clark, 1982), for attempting to restore an aesthetic dimension into the heart of faith.

[24] Von Balthasar, *The Glory of the Lord*, vol. 1, 467.

[25] David Bentley Hart, *The Beauty of the Infinite: The Aesthetics of Christian Truth* (Grand Rapids, MI: Eerdmans, 2003), 308–9, 334, 467.

[26] Brian D. Robinette, *Grammars of Resurrection: A Christian Theology of Presence and Absence* (New York: Crossroad, 2009), 130–48, 150–77.

chosen field of communication. Though now transformed, his risen and ascended body continues in its original connection with the material universe and in primal communication with all embodied persons—in order that they be embodied in the new creation as he himself embodies it.

In effect, a new, expanding field of incarnate relationships is disclosed in the phenomenon of the ascension of Christ as he bears our humanity into heaven, into the realm of life in God. The ascension does not mean disincarnation for Christ, but a new form of inclusive incarnation. The former sphere of fleshly divisions is now relocated, as it were, in a new form of reconciled embodiment (Eph 2:14-22). Its vitality derives from Christ's self-giving love, in order that,

> we are to grow up in every way into him who is the head, into Christ, from whom the whole body, joined and knit together by every joint with which it is equipped, as each part is working properly, promotes the body's growth in building itself up in love. (Eph 4:15-16)

The ascension, then, does not mean a dissolution of the incarnation into the infinite distance separating the divine realm from the human. It is rather an indication of the expansive reality of the incarnation, and of the eternal reconciliation of the divine and the human.

The Ascension and the Face of Christ

Before adverting to the phenomenon of the manner in which Christ "faces" the community of faith, we note the more general case of the face paradoxically making visible the invisible totality of the other. The face resists objectification. At the same time, this "you" calls for a respect and regard, in such a way as to render inhuman any gaze that is just a mere "looking at," as in the inspection of a material object. To see the face of the other—as in eye to eye contact or face-to-face communication—is to find that the center of gravity is shifted. It is not centred *here*, as in the perception of the self-regarding ego (which may well "look through" the other). Rather, the center is *there*, in the other, whose look can stop us in our tracks. In this sense, the face of the other is a commanding presence.[27] It

---

[27] Marion, *Being Given*, 216.

does not reflect back to me what I desire to possess or dominate. It takes me out of myself, into the disturbing world of responsibility, respect, love, and awe. To that degree, the face is not a mirror in which I see myself, but more a window through which the light of arresting otherness breaks through.

As regards the face of Christ and the manner in which he "faces" the church, it must be admitted that the New Testament, neither when speaking of the risen Jesus, nor at any stage in his earthly life, shows any interest in describing his face in any conventionally physical terms. Icons, of course, and the long tradition of Christian art, have sought to serve revelation and faith by expressing the face behind the biblical accounts of Jesus' deeds, words, and relationships with others. The best artistic expression seeks to evoke an experience of the face of Christ as the image of the self-revealing God. Paul speaks expansively of Christ as "the image of the invisible God" (Col 1:15). But the otherness of the transcendent must be allowed to appear on its own terms—looking us in the face—rather than being a projection from our own limited viewpoints.[28] Faith's perception of the face of Christ calls for adoration, self-surrender, and the discernment of his face in the suffering other. It enjoins patience and longing for the final appearance of the ascended One—as in the earliest recorded Christian prayer, Maranatha, "Come, Lord!" (1 Cor 16:22; Rev 22:20).

In that christophanic moment of his return, the true face of Jesus Christ will be revealed, in his identity and his mission, as the crucified, risen, and ascended Jesus, the exalted embodiment of God's self-giving love: "They shall look upon the one whom they have pierced" (John 19:37). In this gaze, faith is aware of the limitations of its present experience in the hope of the future "face to face" vision (1 Cor 13:12). Further, in accord with a bold Pauline idiom, there is already a kind of experience of the face of Christ turned toward the believer in a light from beyond this world: "For it is the God who said, 'Let light shine forth out of darkness,' who has shone in our hearts to give the light of the knowledge of the glory of God in the face of Jesus Christ" (2 Cor 4:6). Faith does not wait in vain, looking up into heaven, but moves out into the world in which the glory of God has been manifest—as it awaits the return of ascended Christ.

---

[28] Ibid., 232.

But then there is Christ "facing" the community of faith in its experience of "being seen through" by the ascended Lord. The Book of Revelation gives a visionary description of the face of Jesus with "eyes like a flame of fire" (Rev 1:14; 2:18), who declares, "I know your works," "your affliction and your poverty," and "where you live" (Rev 2:2, 9, 12, 19; 3:1, 8, 15). He identifies himself as "the living one, I was dead, and see, I am alive for evermore" (Rev 1:18). The transparency of all to him pervades the gospel accounts of various encounters (e.g., Luke 9:47; 11:17; John 1:48). While the economy of privileged appearances comes to an end, and believers who have not seen are declared blessed (John 20:29), there is never any suggestion that believers are invisible to the risen and ascended Lord, or that an opaque screen blocks the church from being seen by Christ.

To Summarize

As a phenomenon of revelation, the ascension represents the culminating moment in the God-given mission of Jesus. As an event, this phenomenon saturates in its intensity and expansiveness faith's vision of the world and its destiny. As a phenomenon of divine beauty, the ascension manifests the inauguration of a new age of hope founded on the glorification of the crucified One. In the flesh and body of the risen and ascended One, our own embodied existence has already entered the realm of an eternal life of communion with God. On the face of the risen and ascended Jesus, faith discerns, in a clouded way, the glory of God's self-revelation and of human existence in the sight of God.

4. Presence and Absence: Various Aspects

Clearly, from what has already been noted, the inherent indeterminacy of the ascension in regard to the routine conditions of earthly existence is not simply negative. Rather, it opens up, from above and from below, a distinctively holy space.[29] In this, the experience of faith is caught up in an interplay of the absence and presence of

---

[29] Thomas F. Torrance, *Space, Time and Resurrection* (Edinburgh: T. & T. Clark, 1976 [pb 1998]), pioneered new approaches to time and space in relation to the resurrection and ascension. See especially 126–39, 179–93.

Christ.[30] It is a space spanning an infinite distance, but in every respect shaped in the form of him who "descended" from above, who once walked this earth, breathed the air of this planet, spoke a human language, proclaimed the reign of God. This boundless space is shaped by him who suffered betrayal, condemnation, torture, and crucifixion—who died and was buried. But this space is not one of infinite darkness, for it is luminous in the light of his rising from the tomb, his subsequent self-disclosure to chosen witnesses, and his eventual ascent to the God from whom he came.

Though Jesus is now absent in contrast "to the days of his flesh" (Heb 5:7), though he has been "taken up" from this world and its conditions, the holy space of his ascension unfolds as a field of vital communication between Christ and his followers. To that degree, the ascension initiates a charged realm of presence in the here-and-now of each life, and of each generation and era of the church. The ascension figures as the "updraft" of God's action in Christ, drawing believers to him in his ascended state—and thereby changing mundane understandings of space, time, body, and presence. The ascended Christ occupies a region of divine accessibility in which all times are now contemporaneous with him, and all places open to his presence. When the ascension of Christ is seen in its relation to the mystery of the incarnation, of the Word made flesh, the result is not to attenuate the reality of the incarnation, but to become conscious of its expansion into new dimensions of time, space, and embodiment.

As regards the singular phenomenon of the ascension, a fourfold negation is implied. First, there is Jesus' departure and his being taken out of sight by divine initiative. Invisibility is the result inherent in the departure of the ascended One into the realm of God. Second, not only is there an empirical negation implied in invisibility and departure, but also a figurative or symbolic negation, in that the overbrimming phenomenon of the ascension exceeds previous symbolic referents to time, space, body, movement, presence, and so forth. Third, there is no conceptual hold on what the ascension of Christ might mean save in terms of his exaltation, glorification, and

---

[30] Robinette, *Grammars of Resurrection*: note the subtitle of this fine work, *A Christian Theology of Presence and Absence*. The interweaving of these aspects impressively pervades the whole book in its treatment of eschatology, resurrection, saturated phenomenon, body, sacrament and selfhood, etc.—even if, as already mentioned, there is little explicit reference to the ascension.

accomplishment of his mission. The disciples' silent gaze upward is interrupted and settles into the joy of inarticulate silence and then ecstatic praise (Luke 24:51-53). The new has been revealed. Jesus' departure means that he is not "here" in the previous sense; nor is he "there" because he is out of sight in the everywhere of divine presence; and though never to be held or possessed or subjected to human control, he has gone to come again. Fourth, the ascension of Jesus to the divine realm "beyond this world" means that he is no longer constrained by the limits of his previous existence, but more, that he has entered into a realm of transcendent giving—a giving and a sending of the Holy Spirit beyond any human capacity to give or produce. These four negativities inherent in the ascension serve to disclose the transcendent "otherness" of God's presence and action in Christ.

Further, the ascension is not to be interpreted just as a *departure*, i.e., as though Jesus abandons his faithful disciples and leaves them bereft of his presence. Departure it surely is, but a departure for the sake of his continuing mission, finally to be realized in his return as the consummation of history. This is expressed in various ways: for example, he goes ahead to prepare a place for those who are to follow (John 14:1), just as it occasions the sending of "the other paraclete" (John 14:26; 15:26; 16:7). Such a departure leads to a space and time of expectation for his final coming.

Though the ascension conveys its own sense of reality and the attitudes of thanksgiving, hope, and expectation, it leaves faith still in the domain of "non-seeing" as contrasted to those privileged witnesses to whom the risen One appeared. The negation of such "seeing" does not require, however, that faith be forever fabricating a collage of visual images drawn from mundane experience as a substitute for its deficiencies. Faith has its senses (1 John 1:1-4) and its experience of the presence of Christ (e.g. John 14:23; 15:4-5; 17:2-21). Though the ascension discloses his incalculable otherness, he remains, and never departs from, the here-and-now of faith. He is *here* in the fullness of who he is, of what he has done, in the accomplishment of his mission—and in the sending of his Spirit, and the promise of his return.

The ascension of Christ is not an inert or exhausted event. Faith is not fixated in recollecting a decisive occurrence in the past with little relevance to the present and the future. Nothing could be clearer from the New Testament data that the ascension of Christ is a dy-

namic reality: in the free dispensation of the Father, the Son's departure is the condition for the Spirit's coming and of his own continuing
presence in another manner—along with the promise of his return
at the end of time.

Rupture

Undoubtedly, there is an element of rupture in regard to Jesus'
previous modes of presence and self-disclosure. Something has ended:
Jesus is assumed into the divine realm from which he came. He is
no longer locatable in the ordinary conditions of life—and death—in
this world. The horizontal range of expectation has been vertically
disrupted. Previous modes of presence and even of self-revelation to
chosen witnesses have come to an end.

And yet with this aspect of rupture, there is an irruptive aspect to
this phenomenon of ascension—the occurrence of an unpredictable
novelty. Whether we term it "revelation" or "epiphany," the ascension
is not an event occurring as a horizontal outworking of any given
state of affairs. In contrast, it is given in a "vertical" and, therefore,
disruptive fashion.[31] There are cognitive consequences: the ascension as a phenomenon precludes any attitude pretending to possess
or comprehend what is being given or revealed. Any predetermined
stock of signs, ideas, and definitions is rendered inadequate and deferred to some final revelation. But what is already given is received
as an ever-original and inexhaustible event in the economy of God's
self-communication as it unfolds "for us and our salvation."

Certainly, there is an ending. But what does this ending consist
in? Jesus is no longer walking the earth, for he is dead and buried—
even though the tomb is empty. Further, the risen One is no longer
with the early disciples as he once was or as he showed himself in
the "forty days" leading up to the ascension. And yet the ascension
does not constrict the freedom of the Christ in revealing himself.
He can still choose to appear to Saul on the way to Damascus, and,
in a different mode, to John on the island of Patmos. Clearly, too,
the ascension does not imply any cessation of Christ's eucharistic
presence, nor does it weaken his assurance of being with the church
until the closing of the age.

---

[31] Steinbock, *Phenomenology and Mysticism,* 9–10.

The sense of ending and departure is always related to the actual economy of salvation. For that reason there is something more than just a rupture and an ending of previous conditions. The ascension marks the accomplishment of the mission that determined the previous presence of Jesus. In this respect, the experience of Jesus' ascension unfolds through phases of rupture, departure, accomplishment of mission, sending of the Spirit, cosmic expansion of his presence, and the promise of his return. The ascension will be the condition for the coming of the Spirit, sent to the disciples by Jesus on his return to the Father. The Spirit will be given, not because Jesus' mission failed, but that it might achieve its goal by expanding it into a new, divinely-determined, universal phase. The appropriate response is not mourning over his lost presence, but joy in the face of all that has changed—in him, in his disciples, and in the world at large (Luke 24:52).

Although he has disappeared and become invisible to sight and palpable physical presence, Jesus' ascent implies an eschatologically cosmic expansion of all that he is, and of all that he has done, suffered, and proclaimed. What was previously located in a particular province of the Roman Empire and in the city of Jerusalem and its Palestinian environs, now implies a new universal accessibility— "neither on this mountain nor in Jerusalem" (John 4:21). The ascension means dislocation in regard to the space in which Jesus had previously lived and died. Universal extension follows on his previous mode of presence in the world. Further, there is no question of the ascension implying merely a form of spatial relocation. Neither God nor heaven are to be measured as inhabiting a circumscribed "place."[32] Being seated as "the right hand of the Father," Christ is where God is, and now returned to the fullness of his power, presence, and glory. As St. John Damascene observes,

> in saying that Christ corporeally occupies His seat at the right
> hand of God the Father, we do not understand the right side
> of the Father in a spatial sense. For in what sense can the
> Unlimited have a spatially right side? . . . By the right side
> of the Father we mean the glory and honour in which the Son
> of God, as God and consubstantial with the Father, abides
> before the ages and in which having become incarnate after

---

[32] Sergius Bulgakov, *The Lamb of God*, trans. Boris Jakim (Grand Rapids, MI: Eerdmans, 2008), 392–93.

His descent to earth, he occupies his seat corporeally after the glorification of his flesh.[33]

Even the time that measured his earthly life is now absorbed into a new "measure of motion" in regard to an open-ended, promise-filled future. From now on, time is radically reconceived; it can be measured only in relation to an incalculable eschatological fulfillment. Time begins anew with the rising of Jesus from the tomb and his ascension to the Father's right hand. It suggests the beginning of a new history. In its unfolding, the whole past of Jesus (including that of Israel and the world itself in which he was incarnate) is now understood as preparation from his return.

Likewise, space is not a three dimensional area of measurement, but a boundless field relative to the universal extent of Christ's presence and action. Christ is at the right hand of the Father. He inhabits a new space and a limitless horizon compared to his previous mode of being. This boundlessness is evoked in the symbolic language of being taken "up" into heaven and wrapped in the divine cloud.

Thus the Spirit will come, Jesus will return, and the Father will act in the proportions of a new space and a new time. At the Father's right hand, on the throne of God, Christ is "the first fruits," the unique representative, intercessor, and judge of a world on its way to redemption: "I am the first and the last, and the living one. I was dead, and see, I am alive forever and ever; and I have the keys of Death and of Hades" (Rev 1:17-18).

The experience of Christ's ascension is destabilizing. The "men of Galilee" needed to be told that there was no point in gazing into the heavens in the forlorn hope of catching a glimpse of a disappearing Jesus (Acts 1:11). They should be looking forward and outward into what God was bringing about. In the unavoidable language of metaphor, Jesus has been "taken up"; yet he is not *up there*, nor *down here below*, nor anywhere else, other than in the "wherever" of God's everywhere. He is, therefore, "with God," "at the right hand of the Father," in that transcendent realm, the heaven of God's presence, power, and saving love for the world (John 3:16). The cloud that receives him out of sight is not a symbol of a celestial nowhere, let alone of a transcendentally distant God. In this respect, faith is not

---

[33] St. John Damascene, *Brief Exposition of the Orthodox Faith*, book 4, chap. 2, c. 1104.

a matter of ever looking up to what is above in a vain quest to locate Christ within the mundane dimensions of this world. It is more the act of looking forward and outward into the cosmic and universal dimensions of the mystery of Christ. It invites faith to apprehend the whole of creation, and to hope for the fullness and consummation of God's self-communication—"God all in all" (1 Cor 15:28).

Moreover, Jesus has been "taken up" in such a way as to promise his return in a similar fashion. This Jesus who lived and died and rose from the tomb will return to bring history to its salvific completion. In effect, then, the ascension disorients hitherto settled dimensions of space, time, and even body. The paradigmatic vision is not intent on fitting Christ into the physical world as it is now known, but, in terms of the Captivity Epistles and the Gospel of John, of locating the whole world, spiritual and material, "in" Christ—in whom all things hold together (Col 1:15-17). It enables faith to contemplate Christ, not in his human form within the created world, but as the one in whom all creation finds coherence, destiny, and fulfillment (Col 1:15-20; Eph4:10). Christ is risen, but not so as to be a visible object within the world. It is more a matter of the world and its history being taken up with Christ and integrated into him.

Presence in the Spirit

The ascension is the focus of rupture and departure in the disciples' experience of Christ, along with the positive features of his mission accomplished and subsequent englobing presence and action. With the coming of the Spirit, Jesus is present in a new way. That does not mean that, now ascended and having finished his earthly mission, he is to be replaced by the Holy Spirit. Jesus continues to act in, and on, his Body as its head, and shares in the divine power over all creation. To stress that the Spirit is not simply a replacement for an absent Jesus is not to deny that the sending of the Spirit was the goal of the mission of Jesus. Indeed, the sending of the Spirit is the actual outcome and fulfillment of the Christ Event. For its part, however, the active presence of the Spirit fills the space made by the ascension and expands the domain of the Word incarnate into the church as the Body of Christ.

Here we note that the phenomenon of the ascension is framed by references to the gift of the Spirit. The promise of the Spirit is inscribed into the mission of Jesus before his death and resurrection. The coming of the Spirit at Pentecost is a decisive event in the life of the church after the resurrection. But even with the outpouring of the promised Holy Spirit, history is still inconclusive: the community of faith must come to a final resolution in the return of Jesus himself in glory. And yet this "other paraclete," the Spirit who is the gift of the Father sent in the name of Jesus, witnesses to him and progressively brings to the consciousness of faith the full extent of what has been revealed (John 16:13-14). The Spirit, therefore, inspires and expands the church's realization of the mystery of Christ as the long history of the generations of faith unfolds. History is also a time of waiting until he comes again from within the "heavenly cloud" that enfolded him at his departure. The cloud is a symbolic depiction of the divine glory into which Jesus has been received. In that heavenly atmosphere, everything he is, was, and will be exists in a new dimension of universal significance and inclusion, to make him present in the "here-and-now" of faith in every age and place.

Ascension and Incarnation

But the vertical dimension and universal expansion of the presence of the ascended Jesus to the world does not mean that the Incarnation has ceased. The rupture of the ascension does not change the identity of Jesus, let alone replace his historical identity with a mythic projection. The ascended Jesus is not rendered disincarnate or disembodied, even though the manner of the incarnation is expanded and the mode of his earthly embodiment transformed. The risen and ascended Jesus still possesses a bodily mode of being. There is no "excarnation," but rather the reach and range of the incarnation grows with the formation of the church as the Body of Christ as history unfolds after the ascension. Who he was on earth, he is now in heaven and ever will be: "Jesus Christ, the same yesterday, today, and forever" (Heb 13:8).

Faith's experience of the ascended Christ contains a new sensibility to what bodily existence might mean. Though Jesus is absent in terms of his previous bodily existence, he is increasingly present in an intimate, vital, and corporeal way, as the present and expanding reality in the Body of Christ is celebrated in the Eucharist. The phenomenon of this Body of Christ is not reducible to the objectivity of an individual biological body, as though the crucified Jesus is resuscitated rather than risen. But what is implied is a vital new field of interactive communication between Christ, the Head of the Body, and the faithful as his members. Though the ascension is a metaempirical event, it does not imply for the ascended Jesus a metasomatic or disincarnate state. Certainly, at such a point, special metaphysical questions for theology need to be asked—as we shall see in a later chapter.

In short, the ascension of Jesus, crucified and risen, does not result simply in a blank rupture in the disciples' experience of Christ. Rather, it opens the way to appreciating him in a new dimension of fulfillment and saving presence.

5. Conclusion

The ascension, therefore, is not simply the experience of Jesus' disappearance. In this respect, it is neither a deliberate concealment on his part, nor a careless loss on the part of the faithful. Faith knows where he has gone and why; and there is no question of faith losing contact with him in his present world-transcending state. As has been repeatedly emphasized: his accessibility is magnified to universal proportions. Faith "sees" him ascending to a properly divine realm from which he will act and from which he will return.

The ascension of Jesus is to be interpreted neither in simple terms of disappearance nor absence. In an obvious sense, he is absent where before he was present. Jesus is no longer accessible as a human being on this planet. Nor does he remain as the risen One episodically disclosing himself to chosen witnesses in the period following his resurrection. These previous modes of presence, however, yield to a new kind of presence in the wake of the ascension. To articulate this new kind of presence requires a rethinking of the continuing incarnation in all its dimensions. It requires taking into account, for instance, the gift of the Spirit, the eucharistic "real presence," the Scripture as the inspired Word of God, the church as the Body of Christ, and even the cosmic concentration of all creation in him.

There is indeed a paradox in realizing that this new universal mode of presence occurs in, and is occasioned by, his absence in terms of all previous experience of him. The paradoxical character of Christ's presence is evident in the New Testament itself and the sacramental liturgy. The presence of Christ is expressed not as a projection of a deindividualized or universalized figure, but in the concreteness of his identity as the crucified and risen One—he who preached the Good News of the kingdom of God and performed works of healing and forgiveness in the particular events of his earthly ministry. The ascension does not mean the celestial dissolution of Jesus of Nazareth, but his glorification as the crucified and risen One. He is not dissolved in the glory of the Father but, by the action of God, affirmed and glorified in the all-encompassing significance of his identity and mission.

It is this Jesus who is ascended and glorified, who is now universally accessible, whose person, words, and deeds—all that he did and suffered—are rendered contemporary to the faithful of every age and place. Such a sensibility pervades the gospels and is continually nourished and refreshed through the eucharistic liturgy. In short, the identity of the ascended Christ does not mean that he is "less" Jesus. Indeed, everything that determined the character and life of Jesus is sealed into his identity as the Christ—and made available to the contemplative faith of the church. There is never any suggestion that Christ is so universalized that Jesus of Nazareth has become depersonalized, or even deindividualized. Although the ascension expands the dimensions of the incarnation to universal proportions, it is always Christ Jesus who is to return as the key and consummation of history.

The complexity of the biblical and historical data concerning the Christian experience of what was seen, what is now seen and not to be seen, what appears and what has been concealed, and what is present and absent awaiting final disclosure, provokes a more thoroughgoing attention to the revealed phenomenon of the ascension. It rules out any consideration of the ascension as a nice construction imposed on the experience of Jesus' absence. While reducing the ascension to a projection on the part of the disciples does not cohere with Christian realism, there is certainly a subjective element, a lifting up of hearts and an eruption of hope. The phenomenon of Jesus crucified, the risen and ascended Christ, saturates the whole of the New Testament and Christian life. It works to transform our whole sense of reality, along with the notions of time, space, presence, body, nature, and universe which so structure human experience. With Christ ascended to the Father, history is newly begun.[34] We move now to a consideration of the Body of Christ and the dynamics of the incarnation as an expanding event.

---

[34] Aquinas' exposition of the ascension moves over the fertile middle ground stretching between biblical figurative language and systematic theological analysis. Note, for instance, how he does not exclude change and movement in Christ because he continues to possess a created human nature (*STh* III, q. 57, a. 1, ad. 1), and further envisages that it was not appropriate for Christ to remain on earth since he is no longer subject, as are all earthly realities, to generation and corruption. In him, humanity has entered into a new mode of existence (see *STh* III, q. 57, a. 1).

Chapter 4

The Body of the Ascended Christ and the Expanding Incarnation

For Christian faith, the incarnation is a singular, constitutive event: "for in him the whole fullness of deity [*theototes*] dwells bodily [*somatikos*]" (Col 2:9;[1] see also John 1:14). To communicate its significance, many kinds of expression come into play—as in the languages of metaphor, symbol, sacrament, devotion, and spirituality, art and moral praxis. More radically still, the incarnational character of God's self-communication in Christ pervades the whole paschal mystery of the life, death, resurrection, ascension, and return of Jesus Christ. The crucifixion terminated Christ's physical life on this earth. The empty tomb leaves a blank, ambiguous space, and the time of privileged "seeings" of the risen One ended with Paul. When on so many counts the risen Jesus is invisible, his ascension seems to establish a further level of invisibility so as to remove him completely from the terrestrial realm and into a heavenly cloud that takes him "out of sight"(Acts 1:9).[2] The two heavenly figures persuade the disciples that from then on, there is a more important agenda than looking up to heaven.

---

[1] Note the two hapax legomena, *theototes* and *somatikos*.

[2] My book, Anthony J. Kelly, *The Resurrection Effect: Transforming Christian Life and Thought* (Maryknoll, NY: Orbis Books, 2008) made a point, but its provocative argument would have been more effective had it taken greater account of the incarnational significance of the ascension. The same goes for an otherwise excellent and much larger book written at the same time by Brian D. Robinette, *Grammars of Resurrection: A Christian Theology of Presence and Absence* (New York: Crossroad, 2009).

A question stirs: does faith in Christ now so follow him into the beyond as to be reduced to a mere memory of him who has irreversibly disappeared from this earthly realm? He may be recalled certainly as an example to follow, and contemplated through the creativity of Christian art and in meditations inspired by the Spirit, but is that the result of the ascension? To put this in another way: has Christ's resurrection and ascension come to mean that he is now in a disembodied state, and that the former reality of the incarnation is true only in a diminished sense?[3]

Such questions are elemental, and they provoke many possible answers. An illuminating perspective comes from thinking of the incarnation as an unfolding event—vertically, in the ascension; and horizontally, through Christ's embodiment in the church, his Body growing throughout history. God's self-communication does not cease to be incarnational; it continues to be actualized in the church in the particular realism of its being the Body of Christ. Such a statement does not intend to exclude other enriching senses of the church as, say, "communion in the Spirit," or the "people of God." Nor, for that matter, does it diminish the importance of researching data on the church's public and historical institutionality. Nonetheless, this effort to focus on the incarnational realism of God's action in relation to the Body of Christ can serve to refine and intensify the sensibility of faith to the reality of Jesus, crucified, risen, and ascended, in the here and now of Christian existence.

Just how this is so is not immediately clear. For instance, scriptural commentaries understandably indicate a variety of "bodily" figures of speech, but the "body language" of the New Testament appears to presuppose something more inexpressible, concrete, and communicative.[4] How might this perception of the bodily reality of Christ be related to our present experience of the world?[5] And how does it relate to the historical reality of the church? Theological

---

[3] For a provocative, stimulating treatment of such questions, see Douglas Farrow, *Ascension Theology* (London: T. & T. Clark, 2011), 33–51.

[4] Raymond F. Collins, *First Corinthians*, Sacra Pagina 7 (Collegeville, MN: Liturgical Press, 1999); Margaret Y. MacDonald, *Colossians and Ephesians*, Sacra Pagina 17 (Collegeville, MN: Liturgical Press, 2000).

[5] For an insightful perspective, see Brian D. Robinette, "I Will Be My Body," chap. 4 in *Grammars of Resurrection: A Christian Theology of Presence and Absence* (New York: Herder & Herder, 2009), 150–78.

methods generally guard against any understanding of Christian faith detached from its ecclesial embodiment and setting, even if that does not preclude a consideration of other contexts—be they literary, historical, anthropological, cosmological, or religious.[6] More specifically, faith in the incarnation can never be abstracted from the particular history and ecclesial community in which it is professed, celebrated, and embodied. For its part, the ecclesial Body of Christ necessarily includes intersubjective relationship between Christ and Christians, coming to expression in a communion of mutual self-giving as depicted in the spousal imagery of Ephesians and elsewhere.[7] Still, a question continues to niggle: to what extent has the ecclesial reality of the Body of Christ been attenuated by the profusion of metaphorical figurations of the church, so as itself to be understood in increasingly figurative and less intentionally incarnational terms?

And then, beyond the ecclesial question of the reality of the Body of Christ, there is a range of eschatological questions regarding the materiality of Christ's Body and its relationship to a transformed universe.[8] For instance, in the solemn declaration of the dogma of the assumption of our Lady in 1950, the intentionality of faith has hurried past its powers of expression—a particular challenge for Catholic theology. If Mary is declared to be assumed, body and soul, into heaven, the authority of the Catholic Church is thereby committed to a view of materiality, corporeality, and physicality in a sense that is as yet beyond our powers of expression, in either conceptual or even imaginative terms. Still, as we shall elaborate in a later chapter, the Eucharist is the paradigmatic moment of the ongoing life of the church. It is not simply a memorial aiming to recapture the past, nor an extrapolation of the present into an unknown future. It is rather an embodied event in which Christ's past—the life, death, resurrection, and ascension of Jesus—and his future return are brought together in the present moment of faith.

---

[6] See "The Mediation of the Church" in chap. 2 of Louis-Marie Chauvet, *The Sacraments: The Word of God at the Mercy of the Body* (Collegeville, MN: Liturgical Press, 2001), 29–37.

[7] For a discussion of this point, see Paul McPartlan, "Who Is the Church? Zizioulas and von Balthasar on the Church's Identity," *Ecclesiology* 4 (2008): 271–88. In what follows, I am closer to Zizioulas. But even in his influential *Being as Communion*, one might ask whether the Body of Christ is fully recognized, given the emphasis on the trinitarian and pneumatological aspects of communion.

[8] Bulgakov, *The Lamb of God*, 393–98.

The incarnation is necessarily linked to the historical bodily existence of Jesus of Nazareth, and which ended in his death. But there
is, however inexpressibly, the expansion of that incarnation into
those dimensions referred to in terms of his resurrection, ascension,
and glorification. With this expansion, and the gift of the Spirit that
comes from it, the church, as the Body of Christ, comes into being.
The church is already pregnant with the new life of creation and
breathes the life of the Spirit. Ecclesial faith does not haunt the empty
tomb, nor is it confined to the past history of episodic appearances of
the risen One, nor fixed into gazing heavenwards. The time and space
of Christ's ascension is the limitless sphere of the church's present
mission and eschatological hope. The ascended Jesus is present to
his disciples in every time, place, and nation.

When the Body of Christ is understood in its expansive totality, it
includes the whole church and even the materiality of the whole universe. It affects the connotation of two indefinable terms, "heaven"
and "the world," as Oliver Davies remarks.[9] Heaven, to which Christ
has ascended so as to sit "at the right hand of the Father," is not the
"empyrean," a determined locality in ancient cosmology. It is rather
coterminous with the immanent and transcendent presence of God.
Given this divine universal presence operating through Christ as the
"conjoined instrument" or organ,[10] heaven is far from being remote
in some numinous, transcendent sphere. It is defined by Christ's
session "at the right hand of the Father," whence he sends the Spirit,
and so opens up a new field of communication with the world. Faith
lives with the vision of "heaven opened" (John 1:51), the actualization of an ongoing communication between God and creation in
Christ. Heaven is not therefore the realm of pure spirits, but the
new dimension of incarnate communication. It is the sphere of an
unbroken and ultimately unbreakable relationship, in and through
the Body of Christ. Consequently, the Holy Spirit comes not as a
substitute for a past incarnation but the transforming agent of its
expansion. The Spirit, active in the conception of Jesus in the womb
of the Virgin Mary, is working in every stage of the ongoing incarnation

[9] "Lost Heaven" and "Interrupted Body," in Oliver Davies, Paul D. Janz, and
Clemens Sedmak, *Transformation Theology: Church in the World* (New York: T. & T.
Clark, 2007), 11–36; 12–14; 37–59.

[10] See Aquinas, *STh* III, q. 7, a. 1, ad. 3; q. 8, a. 1, ad. 1; q. 18, a. 1, ad. 2; q. 62,
a. 5, ad. 1; q. 64, a. 3; q. 69, a. 5.

of the Word—in Christ's life, death, resurrection, and ascension. It is to our advantage—and even, we might say, to the advantage of the Incarnate One—that the Holy Spirit will come (John 16:5-15). While his death and burial ends his earthly mode of relating to his disciples, Christian believers will now relate to him in a new dimension of his bodily reality through the Spirit. The ascended One does not cease to be present to them: they will eat his flesh and drink his blood (John 6:54-58) in the mutual indwelling determined by his new embodied existence. Because Jesus' risen and ascended life is integral to the expanding event of the incarnation, it promises a new mode of presence—rather than the blank fact of absence. Though Jesus is ascended and departed from this mortal life, he is present, acting, and still to come in a way determined by the economy of the incarnate mode of God's self-communication. Thus, heaven is the domain of Christ returned to the Father, and uniting all to himself.

Then there is the equally elusive term, "the world." It is polyvalent in its connotations. Though it is a zone of opposition to God, the world remains, as a whole, the object of God's love, and sphere to which Christ has been sent as light and life. It is not just the realm of materiality as opposed to the spiritual. Nor is it the sum total of our present understanding, however scientific it might be, of reality in general. It is an indeterminate "given," in every moment, itself an indefinable totality that resists full objectification; it is the milieu in which human existence unfolds, and in which it is embodied.[11] The "world" is our familiar native place in which we locate ourselves, "place" others and "size up" the routine realities of our lives. And yet it is the span of an indefinable and limitless otherness. Theologically speaking, to know the world fully would be to know the full extent of the Word made flesh in it (see John 2:21).

Biblical faith is clear in its conviction that, though Jesus departs from human sight by ascending into heaven, he does not cease to be present to the world.[12] In the narrative presentation of Luke-Acts (Luke 24:50-53; Acts 1:9-11), Jesus' departure leads to a charged field

[11] For a distilled statement, see Jean-Yves Lacoste, *Experience and the Absolute: Disputed Questions on the Humanity of Man*, trans. Mark Raftery-Skehan, Perspectives in Continental Philosophy (New York: Fordham University Press, 2004), 8–10; 36–39.

[12] Mikael C. Parsons, *The Departure of Jesus in Luke-Acts: The Ascension Narratives in Context* (Sheffield: JSOT, 1987).

of communication in which the mission of the church will unfold in history. Though New Testament perspectives differ, they do converge in faith's experience of the risen and ascended Lord. Christ's ascension shapes the horizon within which all the New Testament Scriptures witness to him in their respective ways (see John 6:62, 20:17; Eph 4:8-10; 1 Tim 3:16). There is never any implication that his embodied existence has diminished, let alone ceased, or that his relationship to the world and human beings is disrupted.

In other words, the bodily resurrection and ascension of Christ inaugurate an expansion of the incarnation and its fulfillment with Christ's return to the Father. There begins a new way of relating to Christ seated at the right hand of God, so that Christian consciousness itself expands into another realm of transcendence—for those "whose life is hidden with Christ in God" (see Col 3: 1-4). How this expansion of the incarnation to the upper level of the ascension reshapes our understanding of body, time, space, and cosmos resists any adequate answer, despite some brave recent attempts to address such issues.[13] In current scientific understanding, the very nature of matter itself as quasi-solidified energy is a realm of immense complexity. While it is clear that the notions of time and place characterizing former cosmologies have been long surpassed, even now the meaning of energy and its various manifestations admits no clear definition.[14] Given such imponderables, and the undoubted progress of the physical sciences on so many fronts, the implicit cosmology of much of Christian tradition has been radically called into question. Would it not be better, then, for theology to leave any consideration of the body to science? Would the theologian, considering biblical themes and Christian doctrines such as the incarnation, the resurrection, the ascension, and the new creation, be better advised to leave behind all physical and cosmological concerns, and work to enlarge the domain of the spiritual self and its transcendence over matter? Certainly the incarnation was the original defining event,

[13] Torrance, *Space, Time and Resurrection* is among the pioneering efforts in this regard. From an Orthodox point of view, see Sergius Bulgakov, *The Lamb of God*, 379–403.

[14] See P. C. W. Davies and J. R. Brown, eds., *The Ghost in the Atom: A Discussion of the Mysteries of Quantum Physics* (New York: Cambridge University Press, 1993), 26. For further remarks, see James P. Mackey, *The Scientist and the Theologian: On the Origins and Ends of Creation* (Dublin: Columba, 2007), 192–95.

but now that Christ is risen and ascended into heaven, should not faith be now concentrated in the gift of the Spirit?

In "Lost Heaven" and "The Interrupted Body," two provocative chapters in the programmatic *Transformation Theology: Church in the World*, Oliver Davies emphasizes the importance of incarnation faith.[15] He shows how a new cosmological understanding influenced Western theology at the critical time of the Reformation. One result was the loosening of "the relation between the domain of sensibility (the life of the senses) and the actuality of faith."[16] As the sensible domain became increasingly the field of new scientific exploration, the life of faith began to abandon the material world for a realm of interior subjectivity.[17] As a result, something of the bodily and sensuous experience proper to the incarnational and sacramental sense of faith was lost in the course of the last five hundred years or so. The new Copernican heliocentric cosmology unsettled the cosmological imagination of faith based on a Ptolemaic conception of the universe. That premodern world had imagined heaven "up there" beyond the spheres—to which Christ has ascended, and where his risen body was now located. When such a spatial—and now seemingly primitive—imagination was undermined, both the mind and imagination of modern times were taxed in locating the ascended Christ.

Luther, Calvin, and Zwingli, as Davies intriguingly points out,[18] must be given credit for resisting what they understood to be a materialistic objectivity in the expression of faith. Whatever the case, any form of naïve objectivism would be increasingly under threat from the new cosmological discoveries. If the Body of Christ were to be so localized in space as to be regarded as physically "in" the bread and wine of the Eucharist, so "contained" within the material elements, it is understandable that the Reformers would look toward more subjective and symbolic modes of expression. It is left to a later age, and less polemic times, to consider how the bread and wine—and the world itself—in no way constrict the reality of the risen Body, so that these material elements are understood, rather, as "in" the transformed, and all-transforming risen body of Christ. Those who

[15] Davies in "Lost Heaven," 11–36; "Interrupted Body," 37–59, in Oliver Davies, et al., *Transformation Theology: Church in the World*.

[16] Davies, "Lost Heaven," 11.

[17] Ibid.

[18] Ibid., 18–21.

disagreed with Copernicus and Galileo were demonstrably wrong in thinking that the sun moved round the earth. But, theologically speaking, there is the possibility of an even greater distortion, if the sensibility of participating in the temporal and spatial cosmos of God's creative self-incarnation is lost.

In the realist intentionality of faith, therefore, the still-incarnate, risen, and ascended Christ must not be linked to ancient conceptions of a three-tiered universe, or even to cosmologies that look to the modern Newtonian or postmodern quantum world. Whatever the findings of current physics or the viewpoint of present or past cosmologies, what is at stake is the sense of bodily connection between the still-incarnate Word, now risen and ascended, and our present embodied life in the world. Needless to say, there is no essential theological hostility to, say, quantum cosmology. Notions of singularity, emergence, relationality, the multidimensional interaction of mass and energy, the role of strange attractors, and so on, are points of instructive dialogue.[19] But a fruitful dialogue with science presupposes that faith can and must develop its own sense of incarnational reality. The challenge for Christian theology, then, is to expand the sense of materiality and embodiment implicit in Christian faith.[20] The powerful affirmation of Chalcedon remains: the bodily humanity of Jesus is indeed the incarnation and embodiment of the divine Word. And even after the resurrection and ascension it remains so, even if such dimensions of the incarnation are not mentioned in the classic Chalcedonian definition.

[19] On the subject of Pneumatology, see Wolfgang Vondey, "The Holy Spirit and the Physical Universe: The Impact of Scientific Paradigm Shifts on Pneumatology," *Theological Studies* 37 (2009): 3–37. Vondey argues that Pneumatology needs an up-to-date Einsteinian reexpression in accord with the dimensions of order, rationality, relationality, symmetry, and movement of Einstein's cosmology. Perhaps this is an easier project compared with the Christology of the incarnation: in what sense does it presuppose the incarnation? What exactly are the analogical applications of the above named dimensions to the Christian data?

[20] Davies ("Interrupted Body" 40–43) appreciates that some have risen to the challenge, as in Thomas F. Torrance's *Time, Space, and Incarnation* (Edinburgh: T. & T. Clark, 1997)—even if analogical correlations with science-based cosmological views are, to Davies' appreciative reading, too wedded to the metaphor of height, and so result in a certain remoteness from the incarnational materiality. For a fuller discussion, see Tapio Luoma, *Incarnation and Physics: Natural Science in the Theology of Thomas F. Torrance* (New York: Oxford University Press, 2002).

On the other hand, the "body language" of the New Testament provokes continual rethinking of the reality of the Body of Christ and its relation to human existence in the present world. At the very least, that would mean acknowledging that the incarnate Word has not been "excarnated" by being raised and taken up into heaven. Though he is indeed "out of sight" as far as his physical, historical presence among us as Jesus of Nazareth is concerned, he is not so lost in the clouds of heaven as to be removed from all human communication, dematerialized and dissolved in some ethereal medium. The ascension does not mean disembodiment; and if God's action in forming the Body of Christ in its wholeness is acknowledged, is it not better to admit that it is not Christ who has become disembodied, but that we human beings are not yet fully embodied in him as we are destined to be?

But when we consider the resurrection-ascension of Christ as an expanding, incarnational, and therefore bodily event in accord with God's self-communication to the world, the risen Body does not disappear within a primitively imagined cosmos, nor, in terms of more current physics of matter, is it dissolved in the physical universe—perhaps swallowed into a "black hole" or transformed into "dark matter" or "dark energy." In short, faith in the risen and ascended One does not call for the invention of some new form of celestial physics, more in agreement, perhaps, with what current cosmology might tell us. Though science will, we hope, continue to astound us with its explorations, the humble task of theology is to elaborate first of all an understanding of the event of the incarnation in its totality, and the manner in which this enters the consciousness of faith.

It is not as though the incarnate Word has vanished into nowhere, dimly imagined, if at all, only in an evanescent past, or has been lost in some utterly remote heaven.[21] Theology can here make a positive contribution by employing the quite traditional category of "divine missions." These are understood as the effective projection of the trinitarian processions of Word and Spirit into the created world. The missions are, as the term implies, "sendings"—in that, through the gift of God, the divine Persons come to exist in the cre-

---

[21] Has the theology of Christian existence becomes too "spiritual" or soul-centered in its expression? I think so. The eschatology of an "afterlife" or "separated souls" awaiting the resurrection of the body needs some radical rethinking.

ated world in a new way.[22] The divine outreach of the missions is for the purpose of an "in-gathering" of creation into the eternal life of the Trinity—a familiar and ever productive theological perspective. But when it comes to affirming the reality of the Body of Christ in all its dimensions, there is the continuing challenge of bringing together divine causality and the trinitarian missions.[23] Part of the problem is distinguishing, but not separating, the "invisible" and "visible" missions, as in the Augustinian-Thomist scheme.[24] The "invisible" missions of the Word and Spirit occur in the minds and hearts of all good people in the realm of grace; to that degree they span all space and time. The "visible" missions occur with a specific history in the incarnation of the Word in Jesus of Nazareth, and in the ecclesial outpouring of the Spirit—with consequences for our understanding of Scripture as the inspired word, and the sacraments as symbolized mediations of grace, and so on. That is a valuable scheme, and increasingly so, especially as background for any theology of interreligious relations—and in the present case, for an understanding of the still-embodied existence of the risen and ascended Christ. Indeed, as the cloud of divine glory receives him and renders him "out of sight," it would appear that the visible mission fades into the invisible mission in some sense. It would seem that the disjunction between invisible and visible in this instance is not quite as clear as we might presume. For example, is the risen, ascended Christ connected to the "visible" or "invisible" mission? Is there not a certain interchangeability governed by the actual divine economy—as in the appearance of the risen Christ to Paul and in his return at the end of time (cf. *ST* III, q. 57, a.6, ad 3)? The divine dispensation hinges on the incarnation as the governing principle in this matter, even though that does not imply over-rigid distinctions between the visible and invisible aspects of God's self-communication. We might suggest that a more incarnational appreciation of the expanding Body of the risen and ascended One, set against a horizon of transformation and in a field of divine communication, will lead to a more productive understanding of the dimensions of visibility and invisibility referred to.

[22] See Thomas Aquinas, *STh* I, q. 43, a. 1.

[23] In this context, note how Aquinas follows his treatment of the missions with his treatment of creation (*ST* 1, qq. 43–44).

[24] For instance, see Aquinas, *ST* 1, q. 43, aa. 2–8.

Dimensions of the Incarnational Event

The following citation from Abbot Rupert of Deutz, writing in the early twelfth century, is instructive. First, Rupert introduces the embodied unity of all in Christ as he ascends, and "rises up to heaven":

> To the one and only Son of God and Son of Man, as to their head, all the members of the body are joined, all those who are received into the faith of this mystery, in the fullness of this love. Thus, there is one single body; it is a single person, a single Christ, the head with the members, who rises up to heaven, crying out in its gratitude and showing to God the church of his glory, "Here is bone of my bone, flesh of my flesh!" and making seen that he and her come together in a veritable unity of person, he says further, "and the two will be one flesh."[25]

Second, this early medieval Benedictine writer directs our attention to the expanding, eucharistic reality of the flesh of Christ:

> Yes, there is a great mystery. The flesh of Christ which, before the passion, was the flesh of the sole Word of God, has so expanded by the Passion, it is so increased, and it has so filled the universe that all the elect who were from the beginning of the world or will live to the last among them, by the action of this sacrament that makes of them a new dough, he brings together in one Church where God and man are eternally united.[26]

Third, Rupert emphasises the paschal reality of Christ's transformed embodiment, at once an "ascent" for him and an expansion and an increase for his Body made up of many members:

> This flesh was only at first a grain of wheat, a single grain before it fell into the ground to die there. And behold now that it died, it increases on the altar, it bears fruit in our hands and in our bodies; and while the great and rich Lord of the harvest

---

[25] Rupert of Deutz, *De divinis officiis* 1.2, c. 11 (PL 170.43a–c) (my translation). This quotation concludes Henri de Lubac's *Corpus Mysticum: L'Eucharistie et l'église au moyen age* ; *Étude historique* (Paris: Aubier, 1948).

[26] Ibid.

ascends, he takes up with him right to the barns of heaven this fruitful earth in the heart of which he has increased.[27]

Abbot Rupert evokes an upward and expansive incarnational dynamism. It involves three stages.[28] First, there is "God-with-us" in an embodied, historical, physical, and mortal humanity common to all, even if the singularity of a human existence proper to the divine Word must be acknowledged.

Second, there is the presence of the risen—and still incarnate— Christ. This stage presupposes continuity with the past mortal body of the crucified, and is eventually recognized as such in the postresurrectional appearances. But this phase is transitional. For this second stage is a prelude to a third phase implicit in Jesus' words to Magdalene, "Do not hold on to me, because I have not yet ascended to the Father" (John 20:17). In this third expansion of the mystery of Christ in the ascension, the cosmic proportions of the incarnation are disclosed (see John 1:3; Eph 1:10; Col 1:16, Heb 1:3, etc.). Jesus ascends to become the source of the Spirit who will lead believers into all truth (John 16:12-15). The activity of the Spirit is known in its transformative effects in relation to the Body of Christ—from his conception to his resurrection, and then in a final universal outpouring and animation of the church.[29]

Further, now ascended, Jesus is the Lord of history and sacramentally present, in the Eucharist above all.

Christ's Ecclesial Embodiment

Even when these three stages are given their due, Christian faith is hard put to express, let alone imagine, the whole mystery of the incarnation and its transformative effect. In this regard, there is a

---

[27] Ibid.

[28] On this point, see Davies, "Interrupted Body," 45–55.

[29] Davies gives a fascinating account of Paul's Damascus experience as an encounter with the ascended Christ. Might not we also add the visionary experience of the seer of the Apocalypse? Paul is blinded and cannot eat or drink. He suffers a radical disorientation. But after his vision is "mediated" (Acts 9:12–17) in the community, he is empowered in his mission to be the apostle to nations. When Ananias imposes hands on Paul, he regains his sight and receives the Holy Spirit. Significantly, the church-mediated reception of the Spirit enables Paul to recover his worldly life within the ecclesial body, and he is equipped for his mission to the nations.

cloud of unknowing: the life of Christians is hidden with Christ in God (Col 3:4), though "we are God's children now; what we will be has not yet been revealed" (1 John 3:4). Yet even if knowing is inherently limited, faith has somewhere to go and something to do, for the Christian community lives the presence of Christ "performatively," that is, "in action."[30] Through the mediations of liturgy and preaching, in its missionary outreach and dialogical encounters, in its serving Christ in the neighbor, and in loving him even in the enemy, the church performs and embodies its faith. This ecclesial form of the Body of Christ—a community alive with a diversity of gifts—cannot be bypassed.

In this respect, the church is the historically embodied mediation of Christ. As a consequence, the paradigmatic ecclesial moment occurs in the celebration of the Eucharist as the sensible, sacramental, and relational setting of the Christian communion in the present. The church, then, is not a theological symposium; nor is it a conventicle of mystics. It is, rather, a "live performance" of faith—however amateur and poorly produced it might be—as it celebrates in the Eucharist the focus of its communion and source of its mission. Thus the ecclesial milieu is intimately related to the incarnation.

As the Body of Christ, the church is the historical field of experience, witness, and praxis in which Christian faith is formed, or better, "performed"—in thanksgiving for the gift being given in him who was and is and is to come (Rev 1:4). This calls for a theological understanding of the church as the Body of Christ in more than a metaphorical sense. There is the further realism of the church's incorporation in the crucified and risen One. His Body is the organ of God's communication in the time and space of the world. In the words of Augustine:

> If, therefore, you want to understand the body of Christ, listen to the Apostle telling the faithful, "but you are the body of Christ and its members" (1 Cor 12:27). So if you who are the body of Christ and its members, it is your own mystery that has been placed on the Lord's table; what you are receiving is your own mystery. You say *Amen* to what you are, and when

---

[30] A valuable reference here is Kevin J. Vanhoozer, *The Drama of Doctrine: A Canonical Linguistic Approach to Christian Theology* (Louisville: Westminster John Knox, 2005) with its emphasis on the performative character of Christian faith.

you say that, you affirm what you are. You hear, "the Body of Christ," and you reply, "Amen!" Be, then, a member of the body of Christ in order to make that *Amen* true.[31]

In this perspective, there is no suggestion of the church incorporating the ascended Christ into its earthly reality. Rather, what is at stake is the risen, ascended, and coming Christ incorporating new members into vital union with him as history unfolds within the saving dispensation of God.

Christian "Body Language"

By participating in the ongoing drama of the incarnation, each Christian is a member of the Body of Christ. Each one is an irreplaceable character in a precise "plot" of the divine economy as it unfolds under the direction of the Spirit. At the same time, it calls on the traditions of interpretation expressed in those "actors" who, over the generations, have been gifts of Christ for the fulfillment of his Body (see Eph 4:7-13).

As the Eucharist forms the church and the church performs the Eucharist, a unique "body language" is implied. What this idiom means in Christian terms involves questions of tantalizing complexity.[32] But there can be no adequate response if a reductively materialist understanding of the body is presumed, as the body is what someone "has" in a transient way, a physical organism and an individual physical object delimited by time and space. As a specifically human phenomenon, however, the body cannot be appreciated except as the

---

[31] See Augustine, Sermo 272 ; PL 38.1247, my translation of, *Corpus ergo Christi si vis intellegere, Apostolum audi dicentem fidelibus: Vos autem estis corpus Christi, et membra. Si ergo vos estis corpus Christi et membra, mysterium vestrum in mensa Dominica positum est: mysterium vestrum accipitis. Ad id quod estis, Amen respondetis, et respondendo subscribitis. Audis enim, Corpus Christi; et respondes, Amen. Esto membrum corporis Christi, ut verum sit Amen.*

For a less literal translation, see Augustine, *Sermons 230–272 (III/7) on Liturgical Seasons, The Works of Saint Augustine: A Translation for the 21st Century*, pt. 3, vol. 7, trans. Edmund Hill, ed. John E. Rotelle (New York: New City Press, 1993), 300.

[32] In the effort to *distinguer pour unir*, many distinctions need to be made that cannot be treated here—between body and soul, matter and spirit, person and community, the one and the many, the church and the world, etc.; these are some of the distinctions necessary for a full exploration of what the Body of Christ means.

presence of a personal "somebody," organically immersed in a field of communication and relationships with others. A consideration of the experienced reality of this "somebody" throws light on the "body language" in which Christian faith expresses its distinctively incarnate intentionality in reference to the Body of Christ.[33]

The difficulty in clarifying this is not specifically theological, but rather, anthropological. It poses the question of how the reality of bodily existence and the different dimensions of corporeality are to be understood. A Platonic suspicion of matter can make the event of the incarnation and any expansion of it unimaginable. On the other hand, the infinitesimal scale of the biological body within the immense cosmic process makes any insistence on its physical significance nugatory. Nonetheless, while a reflective faith must continue to build connections with philosophical and scientific worldviews, there is still need for a sensitive receptivity to the specific data of faith, if mutually beneficial connections are to be made. Before attempting any correlation of incarnational realism with contemporary science, theology's first task is to insist that faith be receptive to its own data.

In this respect, recent phenomenological studies can be helpful for theology as it reflects on the resurrection and ascension. Before theology is "faith seeking understanding," it must first of all be faith attentive, not only to what has been given to understand, but also to the way it has been given—as gift from the bounty of the Giver.[34] In this respect, there is much to be learned from the generalized phenomenology of revelation as a whole—the better to allow the "given" to come to our consciousness on its own terms as gift—before hurrying to press it into other frames of reference.[35] If Christian theology does not seek to be receptive to the epiphany of Christ in the flesh, it is dealing with abstractions. Included in the phenomenon of Christ are his risen Body of Christ and its ecclesial expansion, most compactly realized in the celebration of the Eucharist.

The phenomenality—or mode of givenness—of the total Christ Event can be blocked by the narrowly empiricist attitude that tends to understand, say, "my body" as something I "have." It is under-

---

[33] Robinette, *Grammars of Resurrection*, is especially valuable on the phenomenological and theological meaning of "body." See 130–48, 159–77.

[34] See Kelly, *The Resurrection Effect*, 15–23, 24–43.

[35] Rolf Kühn, "Phänomenologische Leibbegriff und christologische Inkarnation," *Münchener theologische Zeitschrift* 59 (2008): 239–55.

stood as one among many physical bodies unconnected to the world of relationships shaping human consciousness. The human body is, of course, a physical and physiological object. It is both legitimate and indeed desirable that it be treated as such, when, for instance, the physician takes one's blood pressure, checks one's weight, or measures heart rate and breathing capacity. The dimensions of physiological and scientific objectivity must be respected, given, for example, the stupendous neural complexity of the human brain.

But the consideration of *somebody* only in this way, detached from personal consciousness, is obscene. To further reduce the body to a sexual object, or a unit of energy in slave-labor camp, or a specimen for scientific experimentation, does violence to the phenomenon. The result is to become alienated from our bodily existence. Moreover, there is something fundamentally awry when theology treats the body of the incarnate Word in this impoverished fashion, that is, as an individual object in a historical, sociological, or biological entity without a consciousness of the divine incarnational *economia*.

In contrast to the depersonalized objectification of the body, a far richer and more realistic approach opens when the bodily reality is appreciated as the "saturated phenomenon" of a personal *somebody*. It is disclosed through a special sense of immediacy and unobjectifiable intimacy in regard to oneself and others. It is useful, therefore, to distinguish the "body-object" and the "body-subject."[36] As body-subject, my body is not merely something I possess, but is rather the field of my communication with the other. The body or "flesh" intimately constitutes the subject's being in the world. It implies possibilities of intimate self-giving and self-disclosure—as in the case of erotic or maternal love. In this sense, the flesh of our embodied consciousness is a field of mutual indwelling, and of being with and for the other. This reaches a special intensity in the eros and generativity of love, one's bodily being is re-experienced in, with, and through the flesh of the other.[37]

---

[36] See Louis-Marie Chauvet, *Symbol and Sacrament: A Sacramental Reinterpretation of Christian Existence* (Collegeville, MN: Liturgical Press, 1995), esp. 146–55.

[37] Jean-Luc Marion, *Le phénomène érotique: Six Meditations* (Paris: Grasset, 2003), 185. John Paul II's treatment of this point is necessarily more general but still with a strong phenomenological emphasis; see *Theology of the Body* (Boston, MA: Pauline Books and Media, 1997) 42–63.

The body-subject, then, is more than its objectification as a physical body in a material world of many such objects. It is a field of conscious interactions, a zone of incarnated relationships.[38] For the body of my conscious being is affected by the encompassing phenomenon of the world, and, in turn, affects it. It is at once an elemental bonding with the world, an immediate exposure to it, an immediate participation in it, and a primal communication within it.[39] Through such bodily experience the human person participates in the world of time and space, and becomes familiar with the creativity, dynamism, and final limits of nature itself. The body, with its senses, consciousness, and imagination is our interactive immersion within a surrounding and nurturing world.

Two Perspectives: Johannine Incarnation and Pauline Embodiment

A phenomenology of the body-subject leads to a theological application in regard to the Body of Christ and its relation to the world. The incarnate Word is still "somebody." Christ crucified, risen, and ascended to the right hand of the Father is not beyond embodied communication with the world—as occurs in the Eucharist, to give the primary example. Christian consciousness is, first of all, receptivity to the self-giving bodily reality of Christ. There is no bypassing the communicative reality of his "flesh" (1 John 4:2). The "flesh" of Jesus, when transformed itself, will be transformative in its effect: "the bread that I will give for the life of the world is my flesh" (John 6:51). From the Johannine perspective, the flesh of Christ is the field of mutual indwelling (see John 6:56). In the teeth of objections to this confronting realism (v. 52), Jesus makes his provocation even more intense:

> I tell you, unless you eat the flesh of the Son of Man and drink his blood, you have no life in you. Those who eat my flesh and drink my blood have eternal life, and I will raise them up on the last day; for my flesh is true food and my blood is true drink. Those who eat my flesh and drink my blood abide in me, and I in them. (John 6:53-56)

---

[38] Marion, *Le phénomène érotique*, 170.

[39] Jean-Luc Marion, *In Excess: Studies of Saturated Phenomena*, trans. Robyn Horner and Vincent Barraud (New York: Fordham University Press, 2002), 100; *Le phénomène érotique* 170, 180–81.

Again, objections arising from a grossly materialistic reduction are met by reference to the realism proper to another realm, that of the Spirit. When his disciples recognize "that this teaching is difficult" (v. 60)—even to the extent of compromising its acceptance—Jesus asks: "Does this teaching offend you?" (v. 61). He proceeds to ask how it would appear if, in fact, he were revealed as establishing the vital link between the human world and the divine realm: "Then what if you were to see the Son of Man ascending to where he was before?" (v. 62). It is on this level of the heightening and expansion of the God-world relationship that the shocking realism of his teaching is to be understood: "It is the spirit that gives life; the flesh is useless" (v. 63). His words and his flesh and blood have salvific sense only in the economy of God's giving and attraction: "No one can come to me unless it is granted by the Father" (v. 65).

For Paul, the Body of Christ is the sphere of the new creation. It implies something more than a sociological metaphor, for it looks to an incorporation of his "members," as body-subjects, into the transformed Body of Christ. Paul pushes Christian consciousness toward a distinctive realism. However this might be articulated, it goes further than any facile metaphorical application. The apostle presents the Christian community as composed of members of the Body of Christ: "For just as the body is one and has many members, and all the members of the body, though many, are one body, so it is with Christ" (1 Cor 12:12). With the plurality and diversity of the many spiritual gifts, "you are the body of Christ and individually members of it" (1 Cor 12:27). The shocking implications of this identification appear in Paul's admonitions against sexual immorality: "The body is not meant for fornication but for the Lord, and the Lord for the body" (1 Cor 6:13). Clearly, a bodily mutuality is implied: "And God raised the Lord and will also raise us by his power" (v. 14). It is sharpened with the question, "Do you know that your bodies are members of Christ? Should I therefore take the members of Christ and make them members of a prostitute?" (v. 15). Paul, as if to answer objections arising from a crude or misplaced notion of biological physicality, makes a vital clarification. Between Christ and his members there is indeed a corporeal relationship, but this in the sphere of the Spirit: "But anyone united to the Lord becomes one spirit with him" (v. 17), so that body is now a "temple of the Holy Spirit" (v. 19). The injunction follows: "glorify God in your body" (v. 20b).

The provocative force of Paul's remarks implies a distinctive realism. Christians must live their Christ-embodied reality, not in some celestial sphere, but in the here and now world of erotic impulses and allure. The body nonetheless does remain the realm of communication with the risen Lord through the power of his Spirit. Indeed, this Spirit exercises a bodily or corporate influence. It is, as it were, the shared breath, the living atmosphere, the vital principle of the Body of Christ, manifested in the profusion of gifts. In this one Spirit, "we are all baptized into one body . . . and made to drink of the one Spirit" (1 Cor 12:13). Thus, the Spirit is by no means a disembodied reality, but the sustaining principle of the Body, progressively understood through physical analogies related to movement, energy, joining, and drinking. The Spirit invigorates the Body of Christ as the vital breath; and the church, as Christ's Body, breathes by the life-giving air of the Spirit.

Both the manifold Pauline senses of the "body of Christ" and the reality of the life-giving "flesh" of Christ typical of a more Johannine approach converge as dimensions of incarnational realism. Both justify a distinctive "body language" that aims to express the expanding and inclusive excess of the Word made flesh as the Body of Christ. Each perspective leads to a distinctive Christian realism. Both have disruptive and even scandalous elements in their respective emphases on the life-giving, bodily reality of Christ's presence. For John, the Word became flesh and dwelt among us (John 1:14); and in that flesh, he lived, proclaimed the Kingdom of God, was crucified, buried—and was raised from the dead and ascended to the Father.[40] For Paul, in Christ crucified and risen, "the whole fullness of deity dwells bodily" (Col 2:9). Both these perspectives—Johannine incarnation and Pauline embodiment—point to one reality: the transformed humanity of Christ. His resurrection and ascension do not mean that he has ceased to be God's bodily organ of communication. The incarnational event expands in a manner proper to the new creation inaugurated at Easter.

An incarnational sensibility to the Body of Christ inevitably strains against abstractly spiritual or intellectualistic modes of interpretation. The Body of Christ is more than a metaphorical social

---

[40] Jean-Luc Marion, *Being Given: Toward a Phenomenology of Givenness*, trans. Jeffrey L. Kosky (Stanford, CA: Stanford University Press, 2002), 239.

"body" of coreligionists, as we have said. The intentionality of faith stretches toward a living reality that is beyond the capacity of figurative speech. Metaphors, of course, come into play, as in the Johannine idiom, "I am the vine, you the branches" (John 15:5); but here, we insist, metaphors are employed to throw further light on an incarnate mutual indwelling. For a theological phenomenology, Christ's Body is the organic field of his relationship to the world. It affects and is affected by the manifold reality of our embodied coexistence in him. Though Christ is the form, goal, and agent of a transformed existence, his risen body continues in its "natal bond" with the world. It expresses the immediacy of his exposure to the world precisely in the process of its transformation in him. Paul goes so far as to say that in his flesh, he is "completing what is lacking in Christ's afflictions for the sake of his body, that is, the church" (Col 1:24). Through their incorporation into the subjective-body of Christ, the members of his Body awaken to the world on its way to transformation. Such is the distinctive realism of Christian corporate existence. It discloses a distinctive sense of intersubjectivity and mutual indwelling within the field of incarnate communication. Jesus prays "that they may all be one. As you, Father, are in me and I am in you, may they also be in us" (John 17:21).[41]

The incarnate "Word of Life" (1 John 1:1) takes the form of a communal existence. This is declared with the vigor of an immediately sensuous and affect-charged experience of hearing, seeing, touching, and union:

> what was from the beginning, what we have heard, what we have seen with our eyes, what we have looked at and touched with our hands, concerning the word of life—this life was revealed, and we have seen it and testify to it, and declare to you the eternal life that was with the Father and was revealed to us—we declare what we have seen and heard. (1 John 1:2-3)

The incarnation, at its transforming apex in the crucified and ascended Christ, is extended into the living corporate form of the church. The members of this Christ-Body are drawn into the vitality of self-giving love. For they are, in Christ, "members, one of another"

---

[41] Michel Henry, *Incarnation: Une philosophie de la chair* (Paris: Seuil, 2000), 350–52.

(Eph 4:25), "for no man hates his own flesh, but nourishes and cherishes it, as Christ does the church, because we are members of his body" (Eph 5:30). Indeed, the Letter to the Ephesians does not hesitate to appeal to spousal love as the most intimate, ecstatic, and generative bodily experience to express Christ's relationship to the ecclesial body. Just as man and woman become "one flesh" (Gen 2:23; Matt 19:6; Mark 10:8), the risen One is one flesh with the community of believers. Upon the prayerful reflection of the first few generations of Christians on the full implications of what it meant to be "one flesh" with the community of believers, an extraordinary development in Christian sensibility took place: the early church's prizing of virginity inevitably led to the downplaying of the married state. But there arose a later recognition of the sacramentality of marriage because, we must presume, of a fuller sense of the incarnate character of the Christian vocation.[42]

Furthermore, the inclusion of the suffering body of our humanity in the eschatological reality of Christ's Body is suggested in John's depiction of the risen body of the Lord still marked by the wounds of the cross (John 20:24-26; see Rev 5:6-9). The risen One is ever the crucified One, in compassionate solidarity with suffering humanity and with the whole "groaning" reality of creation (see Rom 8:18-25). The transformation of Christ's humanity beyond death does not mean disincarnation, but a new form of incarnation. A bodily "mutation" has occurred: "the bread that I will give for the life of the world is my flesh" (John 6:51). By sacramentally assimilating his flesh and blood, given and outpoured for the life of the world, believers are conformed to his risen life: "Those who eat my flesh and drink my blood have eternal life, and I will raise them up on the last day; for my flesh is true food and my blood is true drink" (John 6:55).

In short, Christ's risen existence continues and expands his communication in the flesh. Embodied in this way, he is the focus and source of a new order of relationships for which no metaphor is adequate. The limits of mutual indwelling inherent in the physicality of the body-object are now transformed into a new mode of mutual coinherence: "Those who eat my flesh and drink my blood, abide

---

[42] The radical character of this development occurring in the experience of Christian faith over the centuries is striking. The early church fathers may well have been astonished by a pope in this far later age speaking of the "nuptial meaning of the body." See note 3 above.

in me and I in them" (John 6:56; see 15:4, 6). In this eschatological realm, believers "abide in the Son and in the Father" (1 John 2:24; see 3:24). They begin to inhabit a field of love in which earthly *eros* is subsumed into the *agape* of the divine self-giving: "God is love, and those who abide in love, abide in God, and God abides in them" (1 John 4:16).

To the degree that faith assimilates Christ's flesh and blood and Spirit, there is new sight, hearing, touching, tasting, eating, and drinking, feeling, and indwelling—the new senses of faith, as Origen recognized so clearly.[43] Because of its unobjectifiable immediacy and mutuality, the body-subject of Christ is the zone of an intersubjectivity that "earths" and enfleshes faith's experience of the risen One. Neither a spiritual immateriality nor a sensate materialism is implied, but rather a participation in genuinely bodily life in the world affected by the transformation that has occurred.

Because Christian imagination cannot rest content with a play of metaphors, it must continually seek, in theory and in practice, in its attitudes to life and death, to serve the all-inclusive, corporate reality of Christ: "for you have died, and your life is hidden with Christ in God. When Christ who is your life is revealed, then you also will be revealed with him in glory" (Col 3:3-4). A newly embodied self emerges: "you have stripped off the old self with its practices and have clothed yourself with the new self, which is being renewed in knowledge according to the image of its creator" (Col 3:10). In this renewed embodied existence, believers are offered a new sense of corporate coexistence: "In that renewal there is no longer Greek and Jew, circumcised and uncircumcised, barbarian, Scythian, slave and free; but Christ is all and in all" (Col 3:11).

The Analogical Language of Body

A theologically realistic expression of the Body of Christ necessarily remains analogical. Its language must stretch to compare and contrast disparate bodily entities, that is, different kinds of bodies. But the focal reality in this context is the Body of Christ "in whom

---

[43] Hans Urs von Balthasar, *The Glory of the Lord: A Theological Aesthetics*, vol. 7, *Theology: The New Covenant*, trans. Brian McNeil, CRV (Edinburgh: T. & T. Clark, 1989), 308–9.

dwells the fullness of God corporeally" (Col 2:9). Necessarily, Christian body language calls on a wide variety of analogies, old and new, to develop its meaning. The great saint of East and West, Maximus the Confessor, speaks of the human being as "the laboratory in which everything is concentrated and itself naturally mediates between the extremities of each division, having been drawn into everything in a good and fitting way through its development."[44] More recently, under the influence of modern cosmology, Teilhard de Chardin perceptively remarked,

> My own body is not these or those cells which belong exclusively to me. It is what, in these cells and in the rest of the world, feels my influence and reacts against me. *My* matter is not a *part* of the universe that I possess *totaliter*. It is the totality of the universe that I possess *partialiter*.[45]

With his christocentric perspective, Teilhard insists, "Christ must be kept as large as creation and remains its Head. No matter how large we discover the world to be, the figure of Jesus, risen from the dead, must embrace it in its entirety."[46]

Further, we cannot ignore the fact that today we are all somewhat disorientated participants in the amazing development of the "cyberspace body" of our humanity. Electronic energies are employed to extend not only the senses but also the consciousness of the body-subject itself. Our embodied humanity is in some measure being reformed through the experience of new kinds of communication and a

---

[44] Maximus Confessor, *Difficulty* 41:1305B. See Andrew Louth, *Maximus the Confessor* (London: Routledge, 1996) 19–33. I use Louth's translation. See also, Lars Thunberg, *Man and the Cosmos: The Vision of St. Maximus the Confessor* (New York: St Vladimir's Seminary, 1985), 132–37.

[45] Pierre Teilhard de Chardin, *Science and Christ*, trans. René Hague (London: Collins, 1965), 13.

[46] Cited in Christopher Mooney, *Teilhard de Chardin and the Mystery of Christ* (London: Collins, 1966), 136. While I have been arguing for the unique realism of the church as the Body of Christ, I am not thereby conceiving of the whole universe as his body, even though he is "head," etc., of all creation. I am leaving open the question of what that universal and cosmic headship entails. I disagree with Farrow and Barth in this area, who see Teilhard as dissolving the personal reality of Jesus into a gnostic Christ figure within an evolutionary ideology. See Farrow, *Ascension Theology*, 54–57.

sense of "being in contact" to a hitherto unimaginable degree. It is not merely a matter of information exchange, but an aspect of growing global consciousness and sensibility. Human existence, either individual or communal, previously restricted by the limitations of time and space, now possesses the potential to expand beyond previous limits into new forms of communication, relational coexistence, and community. In this sense, the world itself has become the shared body of our being together. It possesses a kind of electronic nervous system—ideally at the service of human intelligence and responsibility, making for a larger solidarity in world-shaping events, and enabling increasing levels of communication and creativity. Present and future technological possibilities cannot but affect what it means to be a body as a field of communication.

The healthy challenge for theology is to make analogical connections between these global dimensions of the body of humanity and the expansive mystery of the Body of the Christ. Without romanticizing these recent developments—the potential for control, surveillance, manipulation, and self-enclosure remains—human existence has moved into a new dimension of embodiment. It has led to a larger "earthing" or incarnation of the human spirit as it penetrates more deeply into matter and energy and assimilates these realities into its range of being in the world. As writers such as Teilhard de Chardin and Walter Ong noted decades ago, such developments cannot be left unrelated to the event of the incarnation of the Word as it continues to expand throughout history.[47] Our understanding of the Word becoming flesh is extended not only to the evolutionary and ecological world, but also to the electronic or cyberspace dimensions of the world of communication.

To what degree, then, do these developments contribute to our understanding of the Body of Christ? In some analogical sense, what is happening prefigures an ultimate transformation of all things, and suggests something of the new creation. If the spirit of human inventiveness and creativity has so transformed our embodied existence, how will the Holy Spirit, having already raised the crucified One from the tomb and animated the risen Body of Christ, penetrate and transform all creation? This is not the occasion to ponder

[47] See, for example, Walter J. Ong, *Orality and Literacy: The Technologizing of the Word*, 2nd ed. (New York: Routledge, 2002).

on the value of medieval speculation on the *dotes* of the Body of Christ in glory.[48] Still, the experience of the developing world of our embodiment may well suggest a range of analogies illuminating the manner in which all communicate in the one transformed Body of Christ, how all are mutually present in the solidarity of love and in the exchanges of prayer and intercession.

In this field of differing embodiments, the analogical imagination must weave its way between the extremes of a univocity that recognizes no differences in the notion of body, and an equivocity that leaves only a nominal likeness between supposedly completely different entities.[49] It is not as though the crucified body of Jesus of Nazareth, his risen body, and the Body of Christ developing in history have only the word "body" in common, without any overlap of meaning or mutual influence. On the other hand, confusion must result when different orders of reality are not clearly distinguished. The characteristic of analogical thinking is to work within the interrelated field of partial likenesses and unlikenesses. It seeks to advance from the more known or immediately experienced to the unknown or less known. In this present context, the aim is to establish some basic analogical reference to the meaning of "body" in a given field of experience. What, then, is the basic analogate for the Body of Christ to which all other usages of the term are referred?

This is an area of some complication, since the literal and the metaphorical, the physical and phenomenological, the philosophical and the theological can be tangled into a formidable knot and

---

[48] For the gifts of *subtilitas*, *agilitas*, and *claritas*, see *STh Supplementum*, qq. 83–85; q. 95 considers these in relation to the risen Christ.

[49] Some years ago, philosophically minded theologians began speaking of the world as "God's Body." Oddly, in one influential instance of this new univocity of "body," we find no reference to the Body of Christ. See Grace M. Jantzen, *God's World, God's Body* (London: Darton, Longman and Todd, 1984). But even in a more general perspective, the divine Spirit is not a partial principle informing matter as another partial principle, to constitute one more complete reality. God is not a part of anything. In the venerable hylomorphic tradition, the soul is transcendentally related to matter to form the body-person. But God *freely* relates to the world as a theater of divine activity and self-disclosure: apart from the singularity of the incarnation of the Word, there is no question of divine embodiment in creation, whatever the metaphors employed for the divine immanence. Thus, the eschatological and transformative dimensions of the bodily analogy are not given their due. See also John A. T. Robinson, *The Body: A Study in Pauline Theology* (London: SCM, 1952).

frustrate the recognition of a fine weave of interlacing associations. More specifically, in the theological context, there is a kind of fruitful and provocative confusion. Does the Body of Christ refer to the individual humanity of the risen Lord? Does it mean the church as his Body? Does it mean his presence in the Eucharist? Does it turn us to recognize Christ in our suffering neighbor (Matt 25)? In what sense is the Body of Christ not only the form, exemplar, and anticipation of the new creation, but the source of transformation for our present embodied existence—in life and in death? The different aspects or realizations of Christ's Body are so interwoven, that one has a sense of a corporeal field of incarnational communication rather than of separable entities.

Still, in this field of incarnational communication, we can recognize interrelated analogical meanings of "body" itself. From each perspective, be it biophysical, sociological, philosophical, personal and interpersonal, ecclesial, Christological, and theological, the prime analogate for bodily existence will vary. In the field of possible associations, what, then, is the primary instance of body around which other instances gather, because of causal influence or paradigmatic representation? Answers will differ, depending on what consideration is the primary focus. Indeed, the choice of a prime analogate at this point could be so exclusive that the analogical field of connotation could easily collapse into equivocity. Such would be the case if one's outlook were exclusively determined by a materialist, literary, or metaphysical standpoint.

In the present instance, given our particular incarnational perspective, the prime theological analogate is the transformed Body of Christ himself. To it all other instances of body are related, and in some sense subsumed within it. Here it is not a matter of ascending from the data of the natural world of bodies to the Body of Christ as a kind of supernatural entity. Rather, for Christian faith, it is a question of attending to the *donum*, the grace of God's self-revelation in the Body of Christ, and so proceeding to understand embodied existence in the light of Christ's self-embodying action.

Admittedly, this suggestion raises a special problem. Though the Body of Christ is the first in the divine intention, it is not the first in the experienced world of body-objects and body-subjects. Does this mean that an incarnational theology is left to interpret the more known (actual physical bodies) in the light of the less known (the Body of Christ)? Does the analogy of faith—and the consequent

interconnection of the mysteries in reference to our "last end" as
incorporated in Christ—inevitably clash with other versions of analogy based in more or less easily available human experience? This,
of course, is not a new problem. It is usually approached by apply-
ing the axiom of grace healing, perfecting, and transforming the
natural. But talking about the Body of Christ is a special problem.
Can the risen and ascended Body of Christ be related as "grace" to
the body of nature and person, to heal, perfect, and transform our
bodily existence?

The short answer, energized by the affirmative realism of faith,
must be, yes. The elaboration of a longer answer of a theology refocused in the divine incarnational economy remains a question of
some difficulty. One aspect of this difficulty is that the analogical
thinking of faith means dealing not with an individual and limited
object, but with a field of communication. This includes the material
world, the world of body-subjects, the incarnate body-subject of the
divine Word, the church as his Body, and the Eucharist as the bodily
actualization or enactment of our unity in the Body. Moreover, an eschatological reserve is required, expressed in an appropriate *theologia
negativa*: the form of the risen One and what we will be are deferred
to a final vision: "Beloved, we are God's children now; what we will
be has not yet been revealed. What we do know is this: when he is
revealed, we will be like him, for we will see him as he is" (1 John
3:2). There is no escaping the necessary darkness inherent in the life
of faith and hope. Nonetheless, the ascension remains the overarching phenomenon in Christian experience, caught in the updraft of
the Spirit's action in Christ. Still, Christian consciousness has its
own sensibility and connatural sense of reality.[50] In this respect, the
analogical intentionality of faith, rather than trying to find a common meaning between a fixed range of different and discrete objects
in the realm of nature or grace, works within an interactive field of
embodied communication. As an illustration of this point, take this
passage from the Letter to the Ephesians:

> But now in Christ Jesus you who were once far off have been
> brought near by *the blood of Christ*. For he is our peace; *in his*

---

[50] *Quid est ergo credere in eum? Credendo amare, credendo diligere, credendo in
eum ire, et eius membris incorporari* (Augustine, *Tractatus in Evangelium Joannis*,
Tr. 29, 6 [on John 6:29], PL 35, col. 1631).

flesh he has made both groups into one and has broken down the dividing wall, that is, the hostility between us. He has abolished the law with its commandments and ordinances, that he might create in himself *one new humanity* in place of two, thus making peace, and might reconcile both groups to God *in one body* through the cross, thus putting to death that hostility through it. And so he came and proclaimed peace to those who were near, for both of us have access *in one Spirit* to the Father. (Eph 2:13-18 [my emphasis])

Given the density of such a statement, theology faces a sense of inevitable defeat in its search for adequate categories to express the incarnational sensibility of faith in all its dimensions. The problem lies in being distracted—or abstracted—into the profusion of the different juridical, sacrificial, social, spatial, and vital metaphors that are in play in this text. Nonetheless, the "blood of Christ" has been shed and now is sacramentally consumed in the Eucharist as "our spiritual drink." The "flesh" of Christ is presented as the form of healing in which the religiously and culturally estranged are united. Christ himself is the form and goal of "one new humanity" living in receptivity to the self-giving of God. This gifted, pacific humanity is realized in, and indeed nourished by, the crucified body of the Lord, so that the vital principle of the Body, "the one Spirit," can be shared by all in their free access to the Father. Here and elsewhere, the Body and Spirit are never played off against each other, but exist in a positive reciprocity: the more of the Body, the more there is of the Spirit; and the more there is of this one Spirit, the more believers are united in the Body.

This passage evidences a particular realism in terms of time, space, and emerging form. In terms of time, "now" is a moment in a great turning point of reconciliation that has occurred "in Christ" through his self-offering on the cross. It does not bypass the historical and antagonistic reality of the separation of Jews and Gentiles—"the dividing wall." There is an implication, therefore, of a new space of coexistence, for the "near and far," hitherto living behind a wall of division. Above all, there is a form of humanity-in-progress under the action of God—a present reality and an eschatological goal.

Summary, Conclusion . . . and Further Questions

In all the above we have been arguing that, in the light of the ascension, the incarnation is not limited to the past alone, but is an expansive and inclusive event in the continuing economy of God's self-communication. The conclusion is clear: Christ is still incarnate, and we are already members of his paschal Body. On this point, Augustine's words are notable:

> Christ is now exalted above the heavens, but he still suf-fers on earth all the pain that we, the members of his body, have to bear. He showed this when he cried out from above: *Saul, Saul, why do you persecute me?* and when he said: I *was hungry and you gave me food.* Why do we on earth not strive to find rest with him in heaven even now, through the faith, hope, and love that unites us to him? While in heaven he is also with us; and we while on earth are with him. He is here with us by his divinity, his power and his love. We cannot be in heaven, as he is on earth, by divinity, but in him, we can be there by love . . . Out of compassion for us he descended from heaven, and although he ascended alone, we also ascend, because we are in him by grace. Thus, no one but Christ descended and no one but Christ ascended; not because there is no distinction between the head and the body, but because the body as a unity cannot be separated from the head.[51]

The Body of Christ has its own realistic unity. However, on the one hand, this does not imply an uncritical univocity that would result in a kind of physical monophysitism or "monosomatism" of the incarnate and ascended reality of Christ in relation to our present bodily existence. On the other hand, the Body is not to be reduced to a vague sense of a metaphorical or symbolic "mystical body." Something more vital, more material, and specifically incarnational is involved, especially when the gift of the Spirit is not considered as a substitute for the abiding reality of the incarnation (see John 16:7, 12-15). The rapid advances of science have led to a radically changed sense of matter, time, and space. Such developments un-doubtedly affect the sensibilities of faith in the Word incarnate in relation to the material universe, especially if such faith remains tethered to bypassed cosmological conceptions. The sense of time, space, and relationship that is intrinsic to the Body of Christ, with

---

[51] Augustine, *Sermo de Ascensione Domini*, Mai 98, 1–7: PLS 2, 429–495.

the assurance of a critical Christian faith, have the confidence to resist conceptions of reality already structured in a nontheological or even an antitheological manner. Christian sensibility to the full reality of the incarnation must keep its own assurance, and not veer toward a new kind of Docetism. On the other hand, a renewed appreciation of the incarnational event and the unfolding mystery of the Body of Christ can fruitfully confront the "soul-less body" of materialistic modernity, and, for that matter, the "bodiless soul" of a rootless postmodernity.

Many further questions need be faced if we are to appreciate the expanding character of the incarnation. It might be that a satisfactory answer will be beyond the epistemic capabilities and imagination of our age. Perhaps the ascension cannot be given its due. Perhaps there are some understandings of the Body of Christ that may well be reserved to those most fully transformed into him. For the rest of us, we must be alert to the point of convergence of many aspects of faith: the risen and ascended Lord already fills the universe; and through the Eucharist, forms the Body of Christ as the dwelling place of God: heaven is opened (John 1:51).

We move now to a consideration of Eucharist and the church as affected by the ascension—in an interplay of presence and absence.

Chapter 5

The Ascension and the Eucharist
Real Absence and Real Presence

The incarnation in relation to the ascension is an expanding event, yet with a particular focus in the Eucharist. The relationship of the ascension to the Eucharist, however, is not immediately obvious. Down-to-earth believers might say, "Well, the ascension means that Jesus is not here and that he is gone to heaven. But he *is* here in the Eucharist, really present on the altar, received in Holy Communion, and prayerfully reverenced in the tabernacle—and that's at least a good substitute for the time being." Such a response makes immediate sense, and is nourished by many forms of intense eucharistic devotion. But a distortion can creep in if there is no connection made between the Eucharist—and even the Real Presence—and the ascended Christ. There is a mentality that envisages Christ as somehow "contained" in the Eucharist. The attention of the faithful is so concentrated on a single issue that a larger frame of reference is forgotten.

For example, even given the Real Presence, the ascension of Christ must mean that there is a certain "real absence," even in regard to the Real Presence. Neither the church nor the Eucharist "contain" Christ, for he is the One who contains all things. We must remember that it is only in the wake of Christ's ascension that the Eucharist is the sacrament that it is.[1] He "fills all things" (Eph 4:10), and all

---

[1] Douglas Farrow, *Ascension Theology* (London: T. &T. Clark International, 2011), 64–70, is good here in his expression of the two-way connection between the ascension and the Eucharist. But such a connection is harder to find among Evangelical scholars. For example, in the otherwise excellent article, Kelly M. Kapic and

creation is subject to him, so that even the lowly earthly elements of bread and wine, transformed by the Spirit, can achieve their final reality by being changed into his Body and Blood for the sustenance of the church. In other words, the Eucharist is not a substitute for the ascended and departed Jesus. Rather, his ascension, with its present implications of Christ filling all things, being lifted above all creation, and promising to come again, finds its earthly expression in the sacrament of the Eucharist.

The Eucharist in turn guides our thinking about the ascension.[2] Nearly eighteen hundred years ago, Irenaeus of Lyons, dealing with Gnosticism, laid down a basic rule for every age of the church: "Our way of thinking is attuned to the Eucharist; and the Eucharist in turn confirms our way of thinking."[3] Thus, the Eucharist provides a basic criterion in reflecting more deeply on what the ascension of Christ might mean. It is not simply a memorial intent on recapturing the past, nor an extrapolation of the present into an unknown future. It is rather an embodied instant in which both past and future are brought to an intense significance in the present. The church is already pregnant with the new life of creation and breathes the life of the Spirit. Christian faith does not haunt the empty tomb, nor is it confined to the past history of episodic appearances of the risen One, nor frozen in a heavenward gaze. The time and space of Christ's ascension is the limitless sphere of the church's present mission and eschatological hope. The ascended Jesus is present to his disciples in every time, place, and nation. And it is against such a backdrop that we now consider the Eucharist.[4]

Wesley Vander Lugt, "The Ascension of Jesus and the Descent of the Holy Spirit in Patristic Perspective: A Theological Reading," *Evangelical Quarterly* 79, no. 1 (2007): 23–33, would have profited greatly by making some eucharistic connection.

[2] On the connection between the ascension and the Eucharist as implied in John 6:62, for instructive comment, see Francis J. Moloney, *The Gospel of John*, Sacra Pagina, vol. 4 (Collegeville, MN: Liturgical Press, 1998), n. 62, p. 231.

[3] Irenaeus, *Adv. haereses* 4.18.5 (PG 7.1.1028).

[4] As a general background to what follows see "Hope's Eucharistic Imagination," chap. 9 in Anthony J. Kelly, *Eschatology and Hope* (Maryknoll, NY: Orbis Books, 2006), 181–200.

1. The Eucharistic Paradigm

The oft-cited phrase found in Vatican II's Constitution on the Sacred Liturgy (*Sacrosanctum Concilium*) refers to the Eucharist as "the summit and source" of the life of the church (SC 10). The path of the community of faith occupies the summit when it celebrates its union with the ascended Jesus, now at the Father's right hand. But as the source, the Eucharist inspires and sustains the mission of the church, which finds in Christ's ascension its true dimensions in anticipation of its homecoming, the final stature of the Body of Christ. In more biblical language, the Eucharist celebrates "the opened heaven" foretold in John's gospel (John 1:51)—the communication between God and all creation enacted in the Word made flesh. Caught up in the updraft of his ascension, the Eucharist of the church is both a gathering in and a going out, a communion and a mission, a thanksgiving and a hope, an enactment of Christ's presence, and a hope for his final return, as the life of faith opens out to the full measure of the mystery of Christ. By receiving the Body and Blood of the Lord, Christians lift up their hearts and "seek the things that are above, where Christ is, seated as the right hand of God" (Col 3:1).

The sacramental economy reaches its paradigmatic form in the Eucharist. The risen Lord takes representative fragments of creation, the elements of our earthly reality which nature and history have combined to produce, to transform them into something more in anticipation of a new totality: "*This* is my body; this is my blood . . ." Jesus' transforming identification with the matter of our world is continued through history as the Eucharist is celebrated: "Do this in memory of me." In effect, Christ invites his followers to connect with the created cosmos as he has done and continues to do. By receiving the eucharistic gift of his Body and Blood, we are in fact claiming this world as our own in the way that the ascended Christ already possesses it.[5] By assuming our humanity, the divine Word makes his own the world and universe to which that humanity is essentially related. In his ascension, that humanity and that world are now irrevocably with God in the glory of a new existence. In this respect, Christian identity grows to an immeasurably larger selfhood as the Eucharist celebrates the expansive event of the incarnation as

[5] See Kelly, *Eschatology and Hope*, 187–92.

it unites the world and heaven understood as the realm of God. But the ascension does not mean disembodiment. Even when considering God's action forming the Body of Christ in its wholeness, it is not Christ who has become disembodied, but we human beings are not yet fully embodied in him as we are destined to be.

The Eucharist, then, is the master symbol within the sacramental life of the church. It is expressive of the whole mystery of Christ and of our participation in it—the essential effect of the paschal event enacted in the death, resurrection, and ascension of Christ. The identity of Christ, the Word made flesh, overflows into the corporate identity of the church as the Body of Christ, in the daily enactment of his words, "Do this in remembrance of me" (Luke 22:19). In its expanding impact, the mission of Christ comes to a certain conclusion with the ending of the "visible mission of the Word," as Jesus ascends into heaven.

And yet, there is no mere ending or departure. The church invokes Christ present in the Eucharist, as the one who was, and is, and is to come: "Come, Lord Jesus!" (Rev 22:20). The hope of the church unfolds in anticipation of his return. It lives with the awareness of existing only by the gift of God, not from human planning of any mundane agency. The life and mission of the church are conditioned by the action of God irrevocably embodied in Christ crucified, risen, and ascended. *He* will come again—the Jesus who is the Christ, and the Christ who remains forever *this* Jesus. The effect of his ascension to the Father's right hand is to lift every consideration of the content and manner of God's self-involvement in Christ out of all worldly categories. It reveals that the origin, scope, and influence of this event are beyond all calculation.[6]

2. The Eucharist: Event and Vision

In the Eucharist, faith is confronted with the gift that comes with a giving and from a giver beyond any worldly horizon. Mundane horizons of the possible, the real, and the knowable are interrupted

---

[6] See Anthony J. Kelly, *The Resurrection Effect: Transforming Christian Life and Thought* (Maryknoll, NY: Orbis Books, 2008), 30–32; Brian Robinette, *Grammars of Resurrection: A Christian Theology of Presence and Absence* (New York: Crossroad, 2009), 174–76.

by a vertical in-breaking of a sacramental event "not of this world."[7] There are dimensions of height and depth and breadth, of presence and future inscribed into the paradigmatic character of the eucharistic experience. A gift is given from beyond all human giving, from a giver who is not of this world, yet at the same time deeply affecting our notions of the Creator of that world, of God's self-giving in Christ, of every dimension of the world, and of our being in the world. As St. Paul would put it, "for those who are in Christ, there is a new creation" (2 Cor 5:17). Our understanding of the Eucharist and its relationship to the ascension is not a matter of thinking *about* some religious ritual or even sacramental event, but more a form of thinking from *within* it, by participating in the experience of what is given within the community of the faithful.

As for the ascension, it is the overarching presupposition and backdrop to Christ's embodiment in the church and presence in the Eucharist. The Father's exaltation of Jesus as Lord over all creation does not remove him from the fabric of the passing world; nor, for that matter, is it a magical reinsertion of him into that world as it was. There is a much larger cosmic and incarnational perspective, for in Christ the world has been taken up into the fullness of his eschatological reality. That is to say that the eucharistic transformation of the bread and wine into the Body and Blood of Christ is the real but veiled anticipation of the destiny of the world. The Christ who is really present in the sacrament is the One who is to come in the fullness of time.

The full significance of the whole Christ Event can emerge only with time and within the liturgical conduct of the church, patiently awaiting the future to unfold. The liturgy does not project a range of new possibilities onto the world as it is, but actively celebrates the gift of a world made new, a new creation, for "in Christ God was reconciling the world to himself" (2 Cor 5:19).

The Eucharist emerges from the creative imagination of Jesus;[8] and, in turn, shapes the imagination of the church as it registers

---

[7] For further, more technical elaboration, see Kelly, *The Resurrection Effect*, 32–33, and Robinette, *Grammars of Resurrection*, 67–103. There is, however, little explicit mention of the ascension and the Eucharist itself in this large and otherwise most impressive work.

[8] James Alison, *Raising Abel: The Recovery of the Eschatological Imagination* (New York: Crossroads, 1996), 57–96.

the impact of what has been and is being revealed. The eucharistic liturgy is an entry into the realm of God's glory, however hidden, to be touched by its beauty.[9] A great work of art has an inexhaustible capacity to strike the imagination and to frame the world in a new way, disclosing something other and something more. In this respect, the Eucharist communicates the englobing reality of Christ, not primarily as an object of contemplation, but as inviting to union with him in every aspect of his paschal existence—his life, death, resurrection, and ascension. The reality of his presence transcends the categories and capacities of the world. At the same time, he draws those who receive him to the singular excess of divine self-giving and to the original and ultimate Giver, within a universe of grace.[10]

The Eucharist occurs within the expanding field of incarnate relationships flowing from the ascension of Christ as he bears our humanity into heaven, the realm of life in God. And yet he is still "somebody." Christ crucified, risen, and ascended to the right hand of the Father is still in embodied communication with the world. The "flesh" of Jesus, when transformed itself, becomes transformative in its effect: "the bread that I will give for the life of the world is my flesh" (John 6:51). The transformed flesh of Christ is the field of mutual indwelling: "Those who eat my flesh and drink my blood abide in me, and I in them" (John 6:56). Clearly the ascension does not mean disincarnation for Christ, nor a dissolution of his bodily humanity, nor a reduction of the Eucharist to merely symbolic or commemorative function. Under the action of the Spirit, the Eucharist discloses the inclusive range of the Body of Christ, head and members, growing throughout time. Through the self-giving of Christ in his Body and Blood, and with the enlivening breath of the Spirit (Eph 2:14-22), a new reconciled and embodied humanity comes into being. Each eucharistic celebration is, then, not only a communion in the Body and Blood of Christ, but a moment in the expanding event of the incarnation as the Body of Christ grows in history.

---

[9] Basic references are already mentioned: David Bentley Hart, *The Beauty of the Infinite: The Aesthetics of Christian Truth* (Grand Rapids, MI: Eerdmans, 2003), especially 15–28, and Hans Urs von Balthasar, *The Glory of the Lord. A Theological Aesthetics*, vol. 1, *Seeing the Form*, ed. Joseph Fessio and John Riches, trans. Erasmo Leiva-Merikakis (Edinburgh: T. & T. Clark, 1982), especially 467–80.

[10] Hart, *The Beauty of the Infinite*, 334.

The Eucharist, even though celebrating the Real Presence of Christ, does not aim to show faith his face.[11] The creativity of Christian art arises from prolonged meditation on the gospels, and certainly produces inspiring forms. Nonetheless, the ascension of Christ entails his radical invisibility—whatever the human projections, depictions, and imaginative representations. Further, his ascent to the Father enjoins the patience and hope of waiting for his final appearance, the return of the ascended One—as in the earliest recorded Christian prayer, Maranatha, "Come, Lord!" (1 Cor 16:22; Rev 22:20).

The Eucharist enables faith not to see immediately, but to be in the presence of the One who sees and will return. Then the true face of Jesus Christ, the crucified, risen, and ascended One, the exalted embodiment of God's self-giving love, will be revealed: "They shall look upon the one whom they have pierced" (John 19:37). Faith does not wait in vain, either looking up into heaven or at images artificially designed to distract from what cannot be expressed. Faith in the ascended One occupies the world as it is possessed by him. While faith awaits the revelation of the face of Jesus, the Eucharist communicates him as intimately present to the community of faith, facing it with his gaze, and exposing it to his transforming power. The community is ever "being seen through" by the risen Lord. Thus the Eucharist, in turning faith toward Christ, places the community in the presence of the One who is to come.

3. Eucharistic Time and Space

Against the backdrop of the ascension, the Eucharist opens up a distinctively holy space. It is formed by an interplay of the absence and presence of Christ. Such an interaction spans a limitless height, depth, breadth, and length of time, but in every respect is shaped in the form of him who "descended" from above, who once walked this earth, breathed the air of this planet, and gave himself for the life of the world—in a gift and a giving celebrated in each eucharistic act. The holy space of which the Eucharist is the focus is a field of vital communication between Christ and the faithful in the here and now of each life and of each generation and era of the church. This

---

[11] See Kelly, *The Resurrection Effect*, 35–40.

"lifting up of hearts" toward the ascended Christ is both a Christian imperative and an act of creative Christian imagination.

Christian consciousness expands into new dimensions within the horizon opened up by the ascension. Faith sees the world "otherwise," affected by the vertical dimension of the here and now of every generation and of every individual person.[12] The members of the Body of Christ already dwell with him in that realm of "the things that are above." Our sense of time now stretches forward in hope for Christ's return, and no dimension of space can exclude his "real presence." And so, when the imagination of the church allows itself to be uplifted by the ascension, the outreach of its communion and the inclusive range of its hope keep growing. It cannot pretend that it has attained, let alone contained, Christ in his fullness. He is risen and ascended into an indefinable and divine "above." And yet the unity of the Body of Christ is being formed: "As you, Father, are in me, and I am in you, may they also be in us, so that the world may believe that you have sent me" (John 17:20-21). A great communion extends through, and beyond, all time and space.[13]

As expressing the "updraft" of Christ's return to the Father, each Eucharist is a moment in a new kind of time, reaching its fullness in Christ and stretching forward to his return. Likewise, space itself is

---

[12] See Anthony J. Steinbock, *Phenomenology and Mysticism: The Verticality of Religious Experience* (Bloomington and Indianapolis: Indiana University Press, 2009), 1–27.

[13] Note the following striking statement of Teilhard de Chardin:

> When the priest says the words *Hoc est corpus meum* ["This is my Body"], his words fall directly on the bread and directly transform it into the individual reality of Christ. But the great sacramental operation does not cease at that local and momentary event . . . these different acts are only the diversely central points in which the continuity of a unique act is split up and fixed, in space and time, for our experience. In fact, from the beginning of the Messianic preparation up till the Parousia, passing through the historic manifestation of Jesus and the phases of growth of his church, a single event has been developing in the world: the incarnation, realised, in each individual, through the Eucharist.
>
> All the communions of a life-time are one communion.
>
> All communions of all men now living are one communion.
>
> All the communions of all the men, present, past and future are one . . . ,
>
> *The Divine Milieu* (New York: Harper and Row, 1960), 126.

reshaped in that Christ, ascended and here and now present in the Eucharist, is not an extraterrestrial object to be fitted into the passing form of the world, but rather the opposite. For the Eucharist enacts a sense of that world as existing and finding its coherence and destiny in Christ. For its part, the Christian community is already embodied in this new creation, assimilated to Christ and indeed assimilating his Body and Blood, to become the Body of Christ.

The ecclesial Body of Christ grows within the boundless field of Christ's universal presence and action. At the right hand of the Father, he inhabits a new space and a new time, within a limitless horizon compared to his previous mode of being. And as the foretaste and anticipation of the world transformed in him, the Eucharist is celebrated in the church. If those "men of Galilee" needed to be told that there was no point in gazing into the heavens in the forlorn hope of catching a glimpse of a disappearing Jesus (Acts 1:11), the Christians of every age find him present in their midst, through the mediation of the worldly realities of bread and wine. From the here and now of Christ's presence, eucharistic faith looks forward and outward into the cosmic and universal dimensions of God's saving action.

It follows, then, that the faithful are united to Christ, not in his previous human form within the created world, but as the one in whom all creation finds its coherence, destiny, and fulfillment (Col 1:15-20; Eph 4:10). Christ is risen and ascended, not so as to be a visible object within the world, but so that the world and its history can be taken up in Christ and integrated into him. In this perspective, there is no suggestion of the church incorporating the ascended Christ into its present reality. Once more, the contrary is closer to the truth, for it is the risen, ascended, and coming Christ who is present, incorporating new members into vital union with him as the history of the world's salvation unfolds.

4. The Real Presence and the Ascended Christ

The Eucharist is the work of the Spirit who transforms the offered bread and wine into the Body and Blood of Christ. By bringing about the Real Presence in this manner, the Spirit brings home to the church the new mode of presence proper to the ascended Lord. Christ is not replaced by the Holy Spirit, since it is the Spirit who makes him present in this sacramental form. As the goal of Christ's mission, the coming of the Spirit fills the space, as it were, made by Christ's departure from this world and his ascent to the Father. The Spirit calls to mind all that Jesus is in word and deed (John 16:13-14), and makes him present in the Eucharist as the head and sustenance of the Body of Christ in the world (John 16:13-14). In this way, the incarnation is a continuing and expanding event; the church is formed and the Body of Christ grows. For Jesus has not simply disappeared into the cloud of glory. In the sacraments of the church, his accessibility is magnified and intensified. The Spirit has come, the Eucharist is celebrated, the Scripture is the inspired Word of God, and the church is the ever-growing Body of Christ.

This is to say that the presence of Christ is not the result of a projection from below of a deindividualized or universalized figure, but communion with him in the concreteness of his identity as the crucified and risen One. He is the Jesus of Nazareth who preached the good news of the Kingdom of God and performed works of healing and forgiveness in the particular events of his earthly ministry. The ascension does not mean some form of celestial dissolution of who and what he was, as though the Eucharist means at best a ritual of commemoration. Christ is not, in the Eucharist, less than who he was, nor less present than he was in Palestine *in diebus illis*. The mystery expands. He is now present to all times and places as the crucified and risen Jesus, not only as ascended, but also as the One who will come again as the fulfillment of history.

When faith follows Jesus in his ascent to the Father, into the glory of the utter otherness of God, it meets him giving himself to the church in the familiar signs of the Eucharist. Though the faithful live in the time of "non-seeing," it can still follow Jesus into that other realm, the Father's house of many rooms—already being sacramentally realized in the Eucharist itself (John 14:2). With him and in him, faith already inhabits the Father's house.

By inspiring such a communal and inclusive imagination, the Eucharist fuels the energies of continuing conversion of the church. It must be open to the universal dimensions of salvation represented in the presence of the ascended Christ.[14] Each celebration of the Eucharist is a moment of truth, exploding any sense of faith as a closed circle of possessiveness. The Real Presence of the ascended

[14] Kelly, *Eschatology and Hope*, 201–18.

One eludes all this-worldly categories to confront the community of faith with an awkward reality, that of the objective, transcendent otherness of Jesus. Although he is really present in a sacramental form, he is nonetheless really absent as an object of possession and control. Although he is now present, he is absent as the one who must come again.[15]

To this degree, the eucharistic community is never complete. With Christ absent in the final evidence of his reality, the absence of others whom the community tends to exclude or ignore as beyond the reach of God's redemptive love is piercingly underlined. By continually bringing a community to a point of crisis in its confrontation with the presence, absence, and the incalculable future coming of Christ, the Eucharist nourishes Christian consciousness toward a growing honesty and authenticity. It is a provocation to "remember" the Body of Christ by healing and restoring what has been dismembered through human lovelessness and violence.[16] Summoned beyond the alienations, exclusions, polarities, and ideologies of any given society, the eucharistic community is turned out of itself by the ascension of the crucified and risen Lord, and is impelled toward a more energetic and creative openness to the Other in all others, that it truly be "holy communion." For faith may not settle for anything less than whole Christ. He is more, the One who has come, and is to come, never to be tabernacled in the routines of church life and experience.

In the light of the ascension, the Eucharist is *the* act of imagination which can rightly be termed "catholic." The Greek root words *kat-holou*, "openness to the whole," must be understood in an expansive, communal, corporate, and inclusive sense. What is envisaged is the totality as including each part, and each part as participating in the whole; the community of the all as present in each one; and each one as present in the universal community. In its compact eucharistic expression, faith cannot but register the great difference within the world of time and space that the updraft of the ascension

---

[15] Douglas Farrow, *Ascension and Ecclesia: On the Significance of the Doctrine of the Ascension for Ecclesiology and Christian Cosmology* (Edinburgh: T. &T. Clark, 1999), 1–7, 41–81; and "Presence in Absence," chap. 5 in Farrow, *Ascension Theology*, 63–80.

[16] See Robinette, *Grammars of Resurrection*, 175–77.

has caused.[17] A great act has begun, and is still in progress: "God was in Christ reconciling the world to himself" (2 Cor 5:19).

It is ever intriguing that the most intense moment of communion with God is at the same time an intense moment of our communion with the earth. For "the fruits of the earth and the works of human hands" are not magically vaporized by the action of the Spirit. These obvious mundane elements attain to their true nature in the realm of the ascended One. In the idiom of John's gospel, the bread and wine become "true food and true drink" (John 6:55). They come into their own as the nourishment for life unending in that new order of existence in which Christ already lives and acts on behalf of his Body, the church.

There is the radical cosmic connection of the Eucharist. When "transubstantiated" by the action of Christ's Spirit, the material elements of the bread and wine are changed in such a way as to anticipate the universal transformation that is afoot in every moment. Thus, eucharistic faith is a form of cosmic awareness. To confess the Real Presence is not to encounter Christ as leaving behind the created cosmos, but as drawing it to himself, for he is the center and form of the new creation.[18] In its openness to the fullness of Christ, faith easily integrates into its eucharistic vision an evolutionary sense of the world as God's creation. It envisions the God-given future as actually already embodied in Christ. He draws the world in which he was embodied, and through which he still communicates with his followers, to the consummation already anticipated in him. As he is, so shall we be. Our earth, our flesh and blood, all matter to God's creative purpose. The transformation ahead does not mean that either he or those who believe in him are emptied of what they truly are. The Christ of glory is ever the crucified and risen Jesus, just as the Body of Christ is composed of those united with him in his death and resurrection, and who are now fed with the Bread of Heaven and taste the new wine of the Spirit.

[17] See Sergius Bulgakov, *The Lamb of God*, trans. Boris Jakim (Grand Rapids, MI: Eerdmans, 2008), 392–99.

[18] On this point, see Joseph Cardinal Ratzinger, *The Spirit of the Liturgy*, trans. Johan Saward (San Francisco: Ignatius Press, 2000), 173. Following Teilhard de Chardin's notion of Christo-genesis, Ratzinger remarks, "The elements of earth are transubstantiated, pulled, so to speak, from their creaturely anchorage, grasped at the deepest ground of their being, and changed into the Body and Blood of the Lord."

5. The Vertical Dimension

In order to express both this supremely personal and universally inclusive reality, the Catholic tradition has coined the now hallowed term, "transubstantiation."[19] It aimed to indicate the radical manner in which the bread and wine are changed into the Christ's Body and Blood, even if this defies adequate expression. Such a change is simply unlike anything in nature. At the same time, it anticipates what is yet to be revealed in its full evidence. Understandably, the singular nature of this change tends to provoke two types of thinking, usefully described as "centripetal" and "centrifugal."

By concentrating on the physical singularity of the change taking place in the Eucharist, theology tends to consider the Real Presence in a "centripetal" fashion. Christ, in the fullness of his reality, is present in the here and now of this consecrated bread and wine through the mysterious act of transubstantiation. The focus is on the Christ here present, in this particular bread and wine, and on the kind of change brought about by the utterance of the words of consecration by the ordained minister. The Real Presence of Christ is the central reality of the Eucharist, so that all other considerations converge on that fact. Theology interpreting it is appropriately termed "centripetal."

But there is another possible approach, appealing to a larger context. The uniqueness of Christ's presence in the bread and wine of Eucharist remains unquestioned. But that uniqueness must be related to all the manners in which Christ is present to the church, (see Vatican II, *Sacrosanctum Concilium*)—in the minister, the community, the whole church, in the Word of God, in creation itself, and, of course, in the consecrated "fruit of the earth and the work of human hands."

While both these approaches are necessary, they still need to go beyond the horizontal perspective of centripetal-centrifugal polarity to acknowledge another dimension—that of the vertical. Both the centripetal and centrifugal descriptions of the Eucharist tend to convey a sense of being in possession of Christ as simply present in a monodimensional manner—"horizontal," in that sense. Both ways of speaking lack a sense of the vertical—God's action reaching into the depths and leading to the heights in a manner already realized in Christ now ascended beyond all worldly categories and calcula-

---

[19] See Kelly, *Eschatology and Hope*, 187–88, 192–95.

tions—and yet to be the source of all the graces and gifts that form the Body of Christ (cf. Eph 4:7-13).

A larger perspective would suggest something like this: under the guidance of the Spirit, the physical, the chemical, the biological structures of our universe have culminated, through a succession of transformations, in human consciousness. In our minds and hearts the universe has become aware of itself as vast, wonderful mystery. Within it, we live and breathe, humbly aware that we are not the center or origin of all this great happening, and thankful for the sheer gift of existence, patient and hopeful as it moves us on toward some final outcome. Into this universe, Christ has come—and forms his followers into his Body, celebrating his self-gift in the Eucharist in anticipation of creation transformed. Thus, a richer ecclesiology and a more evolutionary understanding of reality tend to set the sacramental Real Presence in a larger process of transformation. This has its end in a "cosmic transubstantiation," in which all creation is transformed in Christ, and God is "all in all." This way of thinking clearly owes much to the evolutionary and christocentric emphasis of Teilhard de Chardin. Indeed, in his *Spirit of the Liturgy*, the then Cardinal Ratzinger generously notes that the French Jesuit palaeontologist went on to give

> a new meaning to Christian worship: the transubstantiated Host is the anticipation of the transformation and divinization of matter in the Christological "fullness." In his view, the Eucharist provides the movement of the cosmos with its direction; it anticipates its goal and at the same time urges it on.[20]

Implied here is also the dimension of height—the upward direction of Christ now already ascended into heaven. When the horizon of faith is vertically extended through the ascension, it witnesses to that other dimension which the impersonal "objectivity" of science cannot appreciate: namely, a sense of the universe as divine creation and the theater of incarnation. This "heightened" awareness of the universe senses it as a field of communication. God has called it into being as potentially receptive to the divine self-giving of Father, Son, and Holy Spirit. The Father has so loved the world as to give

---

[20] Ratzinger, *The Spirit of the Liturgy*, 29.

the only-begotten Son to dwell among us. The Holy Spirit has been poured out to form in human consciousness an awareness of great mystery at work in the life, death, and resurrection of Jesus. Christ's ascension means a particular kind of absence, but in its very indeterminacy promises a new form of universal presence, paradigmatically enacted in the Eucharist.

6. Eucharistic Re-Membering

By nourishing mind and heart with such mysteries, the Eucharist celebrates the universe as Christ-filled space in the wake of his ascension. The universe—and the human community within it—is already being drawn into the transformed humanity of Christ. The world is being transformed into the new creation through him who is the firstborn of all creation (Col 1:15). Christ is for the universe the all-unifying "attractor," the direction inscribed into its origin, the goal drawing it onward, and the force holding it together—all this embodied in the plenitude of the risen and ascended One.

In accord with Jesus' command, the Eucharist is an act of re-membering all that has been dismembered in the sterile imagination of culture. Its space is shaped in accord with the "opened heaven" of John's gospel (John 1:51) to expand into the all-inclusive cosmic span disclosed in the ascension of the Lord. But that is not to say that the upward unfolding of faith and hope and love must leave the world behind. The way of faith, even as it opens to the height of the ascension, is not an escape from what we are, but an ultimate reclamation of the physical world and its part in the final state of things. In the measure we taste and celebrate the charged eucharistic reality of Christ's presence to the community of faith, the Christian imagination expands to its fullest dimensions. Paul's prayer begins to be answered:

> I pray that you may have the power to comprehend, with all the saints, what is the breadth and length and height and depth, and to know the love of Christ which surpasses knowledge, so that you may be filled with all the fullness of God. (Eph 3:18-19)

The eucharistic imagination envisions the world "otherwise," in its deepest and most hopeful reality. Christ has gone down into the depths in his death, overcome death in his resurrection, and ascended into the fullness of his humanity with God. The Eucharist as the sacrament of Christ's Body and Blood nourishes the minds and hearts of believers both into a hope for eschatological fulfillment and into a present solidarity with all in the universe of God's creation.

In expressing his eucharistic relationship to the church and the world, Jesus is communicating a sense of reality as field of communion and mutual indwelling. His return to the Father has consequences: "And now I am no longer in the world, but they are in the world, and I am coming to you" (John 17:11). They will dwell in the world in a new way, "that they may be one as we are one" (John 17:11)—a new community based in the unity of the Father and the Son comes into being. Jesus' ascent to the Father opens out a space of holy communion and mutual indwelling: "As you, Father, are in me, and I am in you, may they also be in us, so that the world may believe that you have sent me" (John 17: 20-21).

Jesus prays that the disciples given to him by the Father will be transported into a new sphere of existence, so as to be where he is: "Father, I desire that those also, whom you have given me, may be with me where I am, to see my glory, which you have given me because you loved me before the foundation of the world" (John 17:24). In the mutual indwelling celebrated in the Eucharist, the faithful are to receive the gift of a new vision—to behold his hitherto hidden glory (John 17:24a). In this new luminous horizon, their outlook will be determined not by the conditions and categories of the passing world, but by the Father's limitless original love for him. All history and the progress of events in the life of Jesus himself are held together in the Father's timeless love.

By leaving his disciples, Jesus has in effect relocated them. They live now in the heavenly realm of life and communion, glimpsing the "opened heaven" that the first chapter of John's gospel promises (John 1:52). The prayer of the "ascending" Jesus (John 17:11, 13, 24) asks that his disciples accompany him into the presence of the Father as described later in the gospel as "my Father and your Father, my God and your God" (John 20:17).

Each Eucharist is in answer to his prayer, "that they may all be one. As you, Father, are in me and I in you, may they also be in us . . . I in them and you in me, that they may be completely one" (John 17:21-22). By implication, lasting life is constituted by interrelationships of mutual indwelling modelled on the union existing between the Father and the Son. Each one is *in* one another for the life of the other. By being from the other, for the other, and so, *in* the other, our earthly-human lives participate in God's own trinitarian love life.

Though Jesus is ascended, and the change wrought in the bread and wine by the Holy Spirit has no analogy in nature, the Eucharist is not "virtual reality" in any sense. It is a Spirit-inspired form of actual reality, offering the "real food" and "real drink" of eternal life. In this regard, the Eucharist invites Christians to bring together what is so often kept apart—the sense of God, of the self, of relations with others, and of the universe itself. As the sacrament centered on the "real" presence of Christ, Christian consciousness is not drawn out of the real world, but into it. It causes believers to "re-member," to bring together, their fractured experience on all these levels, by joining them to Christ's Body and inviting them to participate in its growth. When Christ is ascended, he is not *here* in any sense of worldly location, but present beyond any worldly measure or containment—as the Lord of all creation, nourishing the church with his very self.

Chapter 6

The Ascension
Out of Sight, and the Eyes of Faith

The way the ascension is connected to the Eucharist and to the Body of Christ more generally raises questions that stir in the depths of faith's experience. Does the ascension mean that Christ is simply now invisible and out of sight? It certainly means that Jesus is no longer visible as he once was. And yet, it is clear for the life of faith, as we have been arguing, that he is present in other ways. How does this other manifold presence affect the consciousness of faith and its sense of his ascension? Is there any sense in which the ascended One reveals himself so as to become newly visible? Though the disciples are bidden not to look upward for the disappearing Jesus, that does not imply that they are deprived of all vision, or that faith ever afterward is blind. Augustine remarks, *Habet namque fides oculos suos* ("For faith has eyes of its own").[1] But how might such a reference to ocular vision be understood? Aquinas expresses a widely received position on the knowing and unknowing of God. Given the radiance of God, our human knowledge of God is vespertilionine:[2] the bat cannot bear the sunlight; it flits through the environment only with radar-like soundings in its dark world. Still, our human state is not essentially nocturnal, even though the way of negation figures so strongly in the experience of the mystics. Nonetheless, however clouded the present state of human intelligence, it already participates in the divine light—in the words of the Psalmist, "in thy light we see light" (Ps 36:9).[3]

---

[1] Augustine, *Epist* 120.2.8 [PL 33:458].

[2] Aquinas, *STh* I, q. 1, a. 1.

[3] Aquinas, *STh* I, q. 12, a. 2.

Questions inevitably arise in considering the apophatic and kataphatic moments in the analogical affirmations of theology in regard to God. In this chapter, however, we will concentrate more on particular questions related to knowing Christ himself in the life of faith.[4] In that respect, can we speak of the "eyes of faith" in some sense?[5] Our assent to Christ is never negated, nor, as faith confesses that he has ascended into heaven, is there any implication that the ascended Christ has ceased to be Jesus. Indeed, he will come again—just as he was seen departing from this earthly life (Acts 1:12).

The first ending of John's gospel, if taken literally, does not encourage the possibility of a positive answer to such a question. The risen Lord, after manifesting himself to Thomas, asks, "Have you believed because you have seen me? Blessed are those who have not seen and yet have come to believe" (John 20:29). But intriguing questions persist. For instance, how does that original "seeing" of the privileged disciples affect the state of the not-seeing faith of later generations which the risen Christ blessed?

This is a question worth pondering, lest the unique appearances of the risen One to privileged witnesses lose their real impact in the whole sweep of the church's experience, and be regarded at best as a mythological expression or as a psychological figment. Furthermore, the "not-seeing" of faith, however blessed, must not be allowed to suggest that faith is a form of blindness or irrationality. Christian discourse permits expressions such as "the eyes of faith" and "the light of faith." While any systematic answer will prove elusive, a developing phenomenology of revelation can well serve to hold in focus the complex data dealing with the polarity of faith's seeing and non-seeing.

When it comes to "apparitions" of any kind, pastoral misgivings are predictable. But such wariness is not meant to translate into

---

[4] For the pervasive "negative theology" of the New Testament, see Anthony J. Kelly, *The Resurrection Effect: Transforming Christian Life and Thought* (Maryknoll, NY: Orbis Books, 2008), 53–60.

[5] Aquinas speaks of *fides oculata: Christum post resurrectionem viventem oculata fide viderunt, quem mortuum sciverant* (*STh* III, q. 55, a. 2 ad. 1): "after the resurrection [the apostles] saw Christ alive with a sightful faith when before they had known him in death." In reference to St. Bonaventure, see Emmanuel Falque, *The Metamorphosis of Finitude: An Essay on Birth and Resurrection*, trans. George Hughes (New York: Fordham University Press, 2012), 149–55.

suspicion of the authentic enlightenment associated with the gift of faith. Nor need there be any implication that the faithful of these later times are left only with ever-weakening and vaguer traces of the original and unique "seeing" on the part of the earliest Easter witnesses. Still, the passage of time sharpens the question: is the life of faith doomed to suffer a slow hemorrhaging of the original significance of "what was in the beginning" (1 John 1:2)? Robert Browning's poem, "Death in the Desert," poses the question, "How will it be when none more saith 'I saw'"?[6]

Even if these are times of "not seeing" compared to the visionary experiences of the earliest witnesses, what might the ascension mean positively for the experience of faith? How does the ascension contribute to the effective unfolding throughout history of "what was in the beginning"? While Jesus is not seen in the glory of his ascended state, there is the immense visibility of Christianity as a historical fact. It contains the classic expressions of Christian faith in its sacred Scripture, its liturgies, its theological writings, and its arts. More deeply still, there is the living phenomenon of Christian faith as experienced in a communion made up of millions of lives. In short, what kind of visibility does the ascension of Christ allow for and inspire? In outlining an answer to such a question, we will present our response under the following four headings:

1. New Seeing—and Being Seen;
2. From Non-Seeing to the Sensuousness of Faith;
3. The Eye of Love and the Gifts of the Spirit;
4. Toward a Phenomenology of Revelation.

1. New Seeing—and Being Seen

If we begin from a Johannine perspective on "seeing," "not seeing," and "being seen," we become aware of the complexity of the issues. Christ gives himself to his followers through the witness of the Spirit (see John 14:25; 16:13-15), through the witness of others

---

[6] "A Death in the Desert" by Robert Browning, accessed October 29, 2013, www.poetryfoundation.org/poem/173008. I owe this apposite quotation to Ormond Rush, *The Eyes of Faith: The Sense of the Faithful and the Church's Reception of Revelation* (Washington, DC: Catholic University of America Press, 2009) where it appears on the frontispiece.

(John 17:23; 20:21), through the word of Scripture (see John 2:22; 12:38; 13:18; 15:25; 17:12; 19:17–22; 19:36–37; 20:9),and through the sacraments of water and blood (John 19:34, with parallels to 1 John 5:8). Phases of seeing, non-seeing, and seeing again interweave within the experience of the "little whiles" that mark the history of faith (see John 16:16-23).[7]

We might delay a moment on the dialectic of these polarities as they are worked out in the Gospel of John. The gospel tells of the pre-resurrection confusion and foreboding of the disciples as they sensed things moving to a violent climax in which Jesus would be removed from them. In their fear of what was impending, they were still limited to the conditions of the visibility of the earthly Jesus. But he meets their forebodings by declaring, "A little while and you will see me no more; again a little while and you will see me" (John 16:16). The puzzlement of the disciples over these phases—implied in their present "seeing" Jesus and then losing sight of him—is dramatically stated (vv. 17-19). In the gathering darkness, they interpret any promised "little time" of absence as the long time of death—when the dead stay dead, and human fate is wrapped in dread and obscurity. Any future visibility of Jesus following his going to the Father is beyond their imagination, as is his future return to them as a source of life beyond the limits of death. In the history of faith, they are not the last to express their present ignorance and impatience: "we do not know what he means" (John 16:18b).

And yet, a great transformation is promised (indeed, it had already occurred for the writer of the gospel and the early community of disciples). The glorification of Jesus will mean a transformed conscious-ness in the disciples: "Amen, amen I say to you, you will weep and lament, but the world will rejoice; you will be sorrowful, but your sorrow will turn into joy" (John 16:20). Previous reference in the gos-pel to a new consciousness connected it to the radical event of being born anew from above (John 3:3, 6; 16:21). Like the event of natural birth itself, this new birth—in accord with the incalculable power of the Spirit (John 3:8)—is an event of unobjectifiable import. There is a new beginning for human existence in another realm in which the

[7] Hans Urs von Balthasar, *The Glory of the Lord*, vol. 7, *Theology: The New Covenant*, trans. Brian McNeil (Edinburgh: T. & T. Clark, 1989), 295; and Anthony Kelly and Francis J. Moloney, *Experiencing God in the Gospel of John* (Mahwah, NJ: Paulist Press, 2003), 297–305.

followers of Jesus are destined to participate. Their present sorrows are not symptoms of terminal distress, but of the travail connected with being born anew to the fullness of life (John 10:10). But here there is a surprising twist later on in the gospel. The sorrow resulting from Jesus' departure and removal from their sight leads to the joy, not immediately of seeing him again, but of being seen *by* him from the vantage point of glory: "So you have sorrow now, but I will see you again and your hearts will rejoice and no one will take your joy from you" (John 16:22).

What is implied is that the disciples will experience the unfolding of a world-transforming event, however anarchic, incalculable, and overwhelming in itself, as taking place under gaze of risen Jesus.[8] Believers will not be found looking into an empty tomb, nor up to a closed heaven, nor into the sightless eyes of the dead Jesus. Their faith will meet the gaze of "the one whom they have pierced" (John 19:37), in the joy of knowing that their hopes and prayers have been answered (John 16:23-24). Despite the in-between time of struggle and conflict, an ineradicable joy of seeing and being seen by the risen Jesus is not moved indefinitely into the future.

On the particular issue of the "appearances" of the risen Jesus and the visionary experiences of the disciples, these occurrences cannot be adequately described as apparitions or visions of a purely subjectivist character. They bear the stamp of an objective and interpersonal encounter in which the subjectivity of the witnesses is laid bare and their perceptions transformed.[9] While reflection on the resurrection appearances understandably highlights the "seeing" on the part of the various disciples, what is often passed over in the character of such experiences is the quality of "being seen through" by him who sees into the heart. We have already mentioned above the Johannine aspect of Jesus "seeing" the disciples after "the little while" of his passion and cross (John 16:22). The Book of Revelation takes this aspect of Christian experience further. The vision of John the visionary attests to an experience of faith more akin to being "seen through" by the One who sees with "eyes like a flame of fire"

[8] See Francis J. Moloney, *The Gospel of John*, Sacra Pagina 4 (Collegeville, MN: Liturgical Press, 1998) for an illuminating commentary on John 16:4–33, especially n. 22, p. 451, on the phrase, "I will see you again."

[9] N. T. Wright, *The Resurrection of the Son of God* (Minneapolis, MN: Fortress Press, 2003), 209.

(Rev 1:14; 2:18). Jesus repeatedly declares, "I know your works," or "your affliction and your poverty," or "where you live" (Rev 2:2, 9, 12, 19; 3:1, 8, 15). Such an experience has parallels in all the gospels (e.g., Luke 9:47; 11:17; etc.), and is implicit in the resurrection appearances. Before the disciples see Jesus, he sees them. And from this experience of being exposed to his gaze and being faced with him, they are empowered as witnesses.[10]

The followers of Christ stand before him not only in what they already "really are," but also in what they are called to be. The resurrection of the crucified is a constitutive event for Christian identity. The transparency of the disciples to the gaze of Jesus is a summons to conversion—especially at the point where faith had been lacking, or had waned or was even dead. Without this personal sense of being "seen through," the witness of others will never be enough, as the disciples found in the resistance of Thomas to their testimony (John 20:24-29), and as the women discovered in reporting their experience to the apostles (Luke 24:11).

In this respect, the gospel narratives, formed as they are in the light of Easter, provoke an attitude of humility. They tell of how, before the resurrection, the earliest disciples had missed the point. They had been consistently slow to understand (Luke 9:45; John 2:22; 12:16; 13:7; 16:4). Although in one sense they had heard the Word, they still needed to be "faced" by Christ in his risen vitality. Even if the economy of privileged witnesses "seeing" the risen Christ comes to an end, he remains ever present as the one who sees into the hearts of all. Paul is eloquent on the transition from blindness to that new form of "seeing" that occurs in "the light of the Gospel of the glory of Christ, who is the image of God" (2 Cor 4:4). The creator of light has "shone in our hearts, to give the light of the knowledge of the glory of God in the face of Christ" (2 Cor 4:6).[11]

The question returns: what kind of visibility is entailed and what kind of vision does faith have? The "seeing," as well as the sense of "being seen through" are clearly aspects of a many-sided experience. Although the most direct form of expression is "seeing" (cf. 1 Cor 9:1; Mark 16:7; John 20:25; Matt 28:17; Luke 24:34, 39–46; John 20:14,

---

[10] Von Balthasar, *The Glory of the Lord*, vol. 7, 119–21.

[11] Stephen T. Davis, "'Seeing' the Risen Jesus," in *The Resurrection: An Interdisciplinary Symposium on the Resurrection of Jesus*, ed. Stephen T. Davis, Daniel Kendall, and Gerald O'Collins (New York: Oxford University Press, 1997), 126–47.

18; 1 Cor 15:5-8), a larger sensory field of experience is implied. For example, there is the disciples' experience of hearing the risen Jesus speaking (Matt 28:9, 18-20; Luke 24; Acts 1:4-8), walking with them (Luke 24:13-28), preceding them to Galilee (Matt 28:16), and of ascending out of sight (Luke 24:50; Acts 1:9). There are instances of meals in which he both eats and gives food (Luke 24; John 21:13; Acts 1:4; 10:41), as well as many other signs (John 20:30) including gestures of blessing (Luke 24:50), his breathing upon the disciples and their touching him (Matt 28:9; Luke 24:39; John 20:17, 27).

In the case of Thomas and Paul, faith in its full sense was not presupposed. Yet these, too, became part of the limited circle of those whose experience was explicitly visual: "God raised him up on the third day and allowed him to appear, not to all the people, but to us who were chosen by God as witnesses, and who ate and drank with him after he rose from the dead" (Acts 10:39-40).[12]

Appreciated in this light, the appearances can be understood as educative in anticipation of the gift of the Spirit (see John 14:15, 25; 15:26; 16:13-15). Jesus bids farewell from within the mundane visibility of earthly experience, but in such a way as to lead to his deeper mode of presence within history itself (John 14:18ff; cf. Matt 28:20). Through this continuing presence, the history of faith is an uninterrupted exposure to God's saving will in Christ, and enjoys the witness of the communal faith of the church. The supposed "objectivity" of the world, ignorant of both Christ and the Spirit, is called radically into question.[13]

An earlier chapter referred to the discrete objectivity of the resurrection narratives in the gospels in contrast with the more elaborate hymnic depictions of Christ as found in the Captivity Epistles (cf. Col 1:15-20) and in the Book of Revelation (especially Rev 1:12-20).[14] Yet any such elaborations would be meaningless unless they are set within the eschatological horizon opening out from the resurrection itself. For the risen One is never an object to be grasped within the projections and figments of the passing world. Evoking the cosmic significance and hidden glory of the resurrection event, the heavenly witnesses associated with the discovery of the empty tomb ask, "Why do you look for the living among the dead? He is not here, but has

---

[12] Von Balthasar, *The Glory of the Lord*, vol. 7, 356.
[13] Ibid., 360–61.
[14] Ibid., 354.

risen" (Luke 24:5). Similarly, at the end of the economy of privileged seeing, they ask, "Why do you stand looking up to heaven?" (Acts 1:11). Jesus comes, goes, and will return again, in a timing and condition that elude all human perspectives.

In short, the original experience of Jesus' self-disclosure to chosen witnesses affects the later faith of the community. Though the life of faith is "unseeing" compared to the kind of seeing enjoyed by privileged witnesses listed—for instance, by Paul (1 Cor 15:5-8)—there is still a multidimensional visual perception. For instance, the "eyes of faith" will be illumined by the Spirit to find their focus through the community's sacramental signs and Sacred Scriptures. Faith recognizes a spectrum of color in the witness of saints and martyrs, mystics and theologians, artists and pastors. It would seem, then, that the original seeing of the chosen witnesses gives rise to a multilayered developing tradition of faith and gives it special assurance. If, however, the visual immediacy of the self-revelation of the risen One to the privileged few were lacking, the later generations of the faithful would lack a historic content and promise—that of eventually seeing with full evidence what has been inscribed into its beginnings.

In this regard, the gifted visual experience of the early privileged witnesses looks beyond itself to the community of faith in every age. Indeed, it looks beyond seeing to the other senses of hearing, touching, and tasting. Aquinas, for instance, insists on the biblical priority of hearing, for, in all revelatory experiences, hearing precedes the seeing—even in the original experiences of seeing related to the risen Jesus.[15] The disciples hear the angels as heavenly messengers or the testimony of the women-witnesses before they begin to see. In the more general case, the hearing of faith is required if it is to lead to the beatific vision and to the kinds of knowing that anticipate it.

There is another aspect of experience that characterizes the incarnational perspective of John. A seeing and touching (1 John 1:1-3) seems on occasion to predominate over the more traditional experience of hearing the word of God.[16] It remains, however, that the experience of hearing is still basic in the economy of faith since, while sight and touch play their parts, they are less able to register either the excess of God's self-giving or to underline the essential

---

[15] Aquinas, *STh* III, q. 55, a. 3, ad. 1.
[16] Von Balthasar, *The Glory of the Lord*, vol. 7, 273.

self-surrendering receptivity of faith. To hear the word of God places the hearer in a profoundly interpersonal context of relationships of call and response which occur over time. Other sensory experiences can slip more easily toward an idolic representation, projection, or manipulation.[17] But no one form of "sensing" is sufficient; hence the importance of the more comprehensive experience of "knowing," so as to include both the seeing, touching, and hearing in the intersubjectivity of communion with Christ in the Spirit (John 16:30; 17:3; 1 John 5:20).

On the other hand, there is a more comprehensive contemplative sense of seeing, an "ocular" or sightful faith—*oculata fides* in Aquinas's phrase.[18] We speak, as mentioned above, of "the light of faith." It is related to the illuminating guidance of the Spirit as, for instance, in traditional accounts of the "seven gifts of the Spirit" (cf. below). While Paul is quite clear about himself as the last in the privileged "seers" to receive the self-manifestation of the risen Christ, yet, as we have already mentioned, he can still speak to the community of Corinth of "the God who has shone in our hearts to give the light of the knowledge of the glory of God on the face of Christ" (2 Cor 4:6). The implication is unavoidable: the visionary experience of the early witnesses assures and enlarges the contemplative experience of the community of the later generations of those who believe.

2. From Not-Seeing, to the Sensuousness of Faith

The sensory field of Easter faith is never adequately expressed in the five senses of our physical organism. Still, they provide a rich fund of analogical expressions in order to evoke the experience of contact and assurance embedded in a love-guided knowledge that reaches beyond the capacities of sight: "Although you have not seen him, you love him; and even though you do not see him now, you believe in him and rejoice with an indescribable and glorious joy, for you are receiving the outcome of your faith, the salvation of your souls" (1 Pet 1:8-9).

Whatever faith's "vision" of Christ is, it must accept that the economy of privileged "seeing" is over, and another kind of experience has begun. In this phase, a privileged kind of seeing is not the

---

[17] Ibid., 274–75.
[18] *STh* III, q. 55, a. 2 ad. 1.

leading experience. That is now best expressed as "hearing," and being possessed by the Spirit given in the baptismal washing and in the eucharistic eating and drinking. Nonetheless, there is still a visual dimension. Knowledge, wisdom, and insight find their object in sacramental signs and in the words of Scripture, in mystical dimensions of Christian consciousness, and in the (disturbing) visibility of our neighbor (1 John 4:20). As hearing the Word of God and tasting the divine reality predominate in the sensory field of faith,[19] there is also a "breathing" of the "Breath of Life," and an inhalation of its fragrance.[20]

Christian faith lives under the gaze of Jesus from beyond and from the witness of the Spirit from within.[21] The void of invisibility left by the departure of Jesus is the space filled by witness of the "other Paraclete," the "Spirit of truth" (see especially John 16:7-15). The one divine economy permits different phases. The presence of Jesus in the flesh, his resurrection and subsequent self-disclosures, his ascension, the sending of the Spirit, and his eventual return at the end of time—these are not essentially unrelated, let alone opposed. God's saving design is not disjointed. These successive phases interpenetrate: the risen Jesus breathes forth his Spirit, and the Spirit leads back to and enlarges faith's perception of Jesus as the truth, the life, and the light of the world. Within this one economy of salvation—of the Word incarnate and coming of the Spirit—the non-seeing of faith, the visual experience of the chosen witnesses and the testimony of the Spirit are factors in the one living tradition, one unfolding event, in which all believers share, and to which all contribute.

The gift of the Spirit is also marked by present excess and promise for the future: "When the Spirit of truth comes, he will guide you into all truth; for he will not speak on his own, but will speak whatever he hears, and he will declare to you the things that are to come" (John 16:13). The Spirit's activities, described as guiding, speaking, hearing, and declaring, are explicitly related to Jesus: "He will glorify me, because he will take what is mine and declare it to you"

---

[19] Aquinas, "Now God is neither distant from us nor outside us . . . and so the experience of the divine goodness is called tasting," *Postilla super Psalmos*, 33, 8 (my translation).

[20] See Denis Edwards, *The Breath of Life: A Theology of the Creator Spirit* (Maryknoll, NY: Orbis Books, 2008), 171–79.

[21] See the valuable section in Rush, *The Eyes of Faith*, 63–115.

(John 16:14). The christocentric character of the Spirit is reinforced in the First Letter of John: "we know that he [Jesus] abides in us, by the Spirit that he has given us" (1 John 3:24), so that "every spirit that confesses that Jesus Christ has come in the flesh is from God" (1 John 4:2). Moreover, the witness of the Spirit of truth is associated with the sacramental significance of "the water and the blood" (1 John 5:8). The presently "unbearable" (John 16:12) fullness of revelation still comes to believers in every age. The witness of the Spirit gives an incarnational, sacramental, and scriptural density to the salvific reality of the divine self-giving grace—even if it requires ongoing discernment in the world of rejection and conflict.[22]

From a Pauline point of view, it is clear that the gift of the Spirit permeates Christian consciousness, for the Spirit of the risen One saturates all dimensions of Christian experience: "no one comprehends what is truly God's except the Spirit of God. Now we have received not the spirit of the world, but the Spirit that is from God, so that we may understand the gifts that are bestowed on us by God" (1 Cor 2:9-10). A new field of communication results: "And we speak of these things in words not taught by human wisdom but taught by the Spirit, interpreting spiritual things to those who are spiritual" (1 Cor 2:9-13).

Faced with these and similar texts (e.g., 1 John 2:27), theology remains somewhat at a loss. Something intrinsically elusive to any kind of rational mastery is at stake. There is a gifted excess—in the gift itself, in the mode of its giving, and in the way it is received. A certain affective and cognitive "feel," "instinct," or "sympathy" is implied in the effusive character of the gift.[23] It gives rise to the tradition of "spiritual senses," as found with different emphases in the writings of Origen, Augustine, Bonaventure, and Ignatius of Loyola.[24] In this respect, the eyes of faith are an aspect of the liveli-

---

[22] For an excellent treatment of discernment, see Mark A. McIntosh, *Discernment and Truth: The Spirituality and Theology of Knowledge* (New York: Crossroads, 2004).

[23] For a valuable exploration of this affective dimension, see Thomas Ryan, SM, "Revisiting Affective Knowledge and Connaturality in Aquinas," *Theological Studies* 66 (2005): 49–68.

[24] Hans Urs von Balthasar, *The Glory of the Lord*, vol. 1, *Seeing the Form*, ed. Joseph Fessio and John Riches, trans. Erasmo Leiva-Merikakis (Edinburgh: T. & T. Clark, 1982), 365–80. For a variety of historical perspectives, see Paul Gavrilyuk and

ness of a new consciousness, a *con-naissance*, "being born with," in regard to him who is the firstborn from the dead into the fullness of life. Christian consciousness stirs with new perceptions marking a progressive interiorization and expansion of the Body of Christ.[25] Thus, the horizon of faith is illumined and enlarged by the ascension of Christ in whom the glory of true life is revealed.

3. The Eye of Love and the Gifts of the Spirit

Such vivid perceptions of Christ in the life of faith imply a certain vision and call on a long tradition.[26] For example, Bernard Lonergan writes of faith as the "eye of religious love."[27] There is a new way of seeing that arises from love, and above all, from God-given and God-directed love: "there is another kind of knowledge reached through the discernment of value and the judgments of value of a person in love. Faith, accordingly, is such further knowledge when the love is God's love flooding our hearts."[28]

Consciousness, affected by the love that has been given, reciprocated, and shared, recognizes the value of believing within the community of faith and being carried forward by its manifold witness:

> Beliefs result from judgments of value, and the judgments of value relevant for religious belief come from faith, the eye of religious love, an eye that can discern God's self-disclosures.[29]

Thus, the love that informs faith not only unites believers to God, but also locates them in the community of faith. Faith is a social bond that gives rise to shared scriptural, doctrinal, institutional, and moral beliefs, expressive of a shared sense of what has

---

Sarah Coakley, eds. *The Spiritual Senses: Perceiving God in Western Christianity* (Cambridge, UK: Cambridge University Press, 2012).

[25] See Anthony J. Kelly, "'The Body of Christ: Amen': The Expanding Incarnation," *Theological Studies* 71 (2010): 792–816.

[26] See, for instance, Pierre Rousselot, *The Eyes of Faith and Answers to Two Objections*, trans. J. F. Donceel and Avery Dulles (New York: Fordham University Press, 1990).

[27] Bernard Lonergan, *Method in Theology* (London: Darton, Longman and Todd, 1972), 119.

[28] Ibid., 115.

[29] Ibid., 119.

been revealed and must now be passed on to future generations. In this shared awareness or sense of faith, faith makes its own the body of attestations, narratives, and judgments as found in the gospels and other writings of the New Testament. That appropriation of the earliest written tradition can hardly be separated from the church's liturgical expressiveness. The common celebration in adoration and thanksgiving of what has been revealed in Christ is the site in which the Word of God, in scripture or proclamation, lives and works its transformative effect. Within the developments of its history, this faith is further focused, and the beliefs that express it are more sharply articulated in the words of the creeds, in symbolic communications, in the witness of saints, doctors, and martyrs, in the rise of theologies, and in the development of the arts—musical, figurative, architectural, and so forth.

By locating the cognitive aspect of faith and shared beliefs in the affectivity of consciousness transformed by the gift of love and shared within the corporate experience of the church, Lonergan is invoking a long tradition represented in the Thomist understanding of the connaturalizing power of charity, and the operation of the "gifts of the Spirit."

The traditional enumeration of the sevenfold gifts of the Spirit includes wisdom, understanding, counsel, fortitude, knowledge, piety, and fear of the Lord. Aquinas presents the gift of grace as saturating every aspect of the cognitive and conative life of faith. The seven gifts are given to enable the graced subject to respond to the movement of the Spirit and to act in a manner that is "beyond the human measure."[30] While the life of faith is intelligible in the hardy world of objective and rational theological discourse, the gifts of the Spirit represent a vertically-given excess extending, or even disrupting, the horizons of reason alone. Intelligence must be receptive, waiting, as it were, on the gift from above, in order to know and act in a way that respects the irruptive and transformative character of the Spirit's action. Each gift is an aspect of transforming grace of the Spirit. Each gift specifies a particular receptivity within Christian consciousness to the Spirit's "supra-rational" action. Consequently, the notion of these gifts of the Spirit leads to a healthy deconstruction

---

[30] *III Sent* d. 34, q. 1 a. 1; *STh* 1–2, 70, 4.

of a one-dimensional, rational, or calculative mode of thinking,[31] while suggesting other domains of spiritual perception.

The Thomist account of the gifts recognizes that there exists a certain strain or dislocation that is inherent in the life of faith. There is an essential cloudiness in its vision and negativity in its mode of knowing—inevitable aspects of "non-seeing." While there is a native aptitude for the pursuit of the good and the true proportionate to this present mode of human existence in the world, such a "connaturality" is lacking in regard to the supernatural end of participating in God's own life. A necessary complement, therefore, to our "new creation" in Christ is found in the gifts of the Spirit in that they attune the mind and heart of the believer to the divine milieu in which faith must now live. New life in Christ is received and integrated into human existence by means of "an instinct and movement of the Holy Spirit."[32] If believers are not given a more lively, supple, and receptive attunement to the Spirit's interior action, Thomas seems to fear that our sense of God will be annexed to—or seduced by—a limited rational or empiricist mode of knowing and acting. A monodimensional rationality would tend to edge out the kind of receptivity and surrender that the gift of the Spirit entails. And so, the God of grace equips faith with a special instinct, enabling it to reach beyond mundane patterns of calculation.[33]

As a consequence, the grace of the Spirit has a transforming influence on Christian consciousness. This transformation is expressed in terms of a new birth, a new identity, and a new level of spiritual activity. For instance, in the cognitive domain, there is given a special "taste" for the things of God, coming in the gift *par excellence*, "wisdom" (*sapientia*, from *sapere*, "to taste").[34] It is at once a tasting

---

[31] See my "The Gifts of the Spirit: Aquinas in the Modern Context," *The Thomist* 38 (1974): 193–231. Admittedly, that "modern context" has exploded into postmodernity just as more inclusive language is now imperative!

[32] *STh* 1–2, q. 68, a. 2.

[33] In the activity of the theological virtues is found the radical condition for the operation of the gifts. The movement of the Spirit is recognized in charity: "faith is about what is not seen, hope is concerned with what is not possessed, but the love of charity concerns the one who is already possessed, for the beloved is somehow within the lover, and also the lover is affectively attracted to be united with the beloved" (*STh* 1–2, 66, 5).

[34] *STh* 2–2, q. 45, a. 1–6.

and an attunement to the reality of the crucified and risen One mediated in the life of the church. It amounts to a "feel" for the totality of the divine economy centered in Christ.[35] Then there is the gift of "understanding" (*intellectus*), implying a clear-eyed perception of the uniqueness of the Christ Event, protecting it from the impressions and projections that would distort its transcendent originality and reduce it to some general class of religious phenomena.[36] The gift of "knowledge" (*scientia*) likewise bears on the uniqueness of such an event, to save its universal significance from being lost in an empty and meaningless contingency.[37]

There is, then, a cognitive significance in what is traditionally referred to as the gifts of wisdom, understanding, and knowledge. They represent perceptions of the incarnational and sacramental realities celebrated in the liturgy, enabling a sense of God's self-communication taking place in and through the familiar elements and words of the world in which we live.

In all this, there is the further gift of *pietas*, by which Christian consciousness lives with an intimate sense of filial relationship with the God who has acted in glorifying his Son and uniting us to him. The gift of "fear of the Lord" (*timor Domini*) brings with it a radical poverty of spirit, along with a reverent sensitivity to the way God has acted in raising the crucified Jesus.[38] In the domain of moral action, the gift of "counsel" (*consilum*) is the special Spirit-guided instinct for freedom responding to God's act in Christ: in the folly of the cross and surprise of the resurrection, all ethical action is concretely affected with a new capacity for discernment. The hierarchy of values structuring any cultural world must have room from a love stronger than death, beyond the world of even ethical calculation.[39] Finally, "fortitude" (*fortitudo*) is an experience of the Spirit manifest in resoluteness in living in the light of the risen victim, despite the violence of a world intent on crucifying what stands in the way of its self-serving projects.[40]

---

[35] *STh* 2–2, 45, 2. Compare with John Macquarrie, "The Seven Gifts of the Holy Spirit," *Studies in Christian Existentialism* (London: SCM, 1965), 246–73.

[36] *STh* 2–2, q. 8, a. 1–8.

[37] *STh* 2–2, q. 9, a. 1–4.

[38] *STh* 2–2, q. 19, a. 1–12.

[39] Cf. *ST* 2–2, q. 52, a. 1–4.

[40] Cf. *STh* 2–2, q. 139, a. 1.

This is to suggest that the more general consideration of the life of grace can be profitably refocused on the gift behind the gifts, namely, the risen Christ himself, the incarnate form, revelation, and source of such grace. With a more christocentric focus, the gifts of the Spirit are not unlike the change wrought in those who had followed Jesus to his death, but then experienced the transformation of mind, heart, and sensibility following on his resurrection. Though Aquinas's treatment of the experience of grace is more generalized, his treatment of the gifts can suggest aspects of faith's consciousness of the risen Jesus in the ongoing life of the church. The resurrection occurs as an irruptive event. It manifests Christ's victory over death, his transformed existence, and his presence and action as the source of eternal life. In him, the new creation (2 Cor 5:17) has begun and a new consciousness derives from it, manifested in the faith, hope, and charity of Christian existence. The excess marking this realm of life is found in the gifts of the Spirit in that they attune the mind and heart of the followers of Christ to the milieu in which the risen Christ is the focus, and the Spirit is the inexhaustible source of the inexhaustible energy and sensibility by which faith must now live. Only through these gifts can the gift of life in the risen One be received and integrated into human existence by means of "an instinct and movement of the Holy Spirit."[41]

Far from destroying or compromising human intelligence and liberty, the Spirit-given "instinct" manifest in the gifts enlarges and completes the Christian's affective, intellectual, and moral capacities. The grace of the Spirit thus looks beyond the calculations of horizontal rationality to endow mind and heart with an evidence, however clouded, of something more—and a receptivity to grace that keeps on being grace, that is, by always retaining its character as a gift of new sight. In short, as the event of the resurrection disrupts the horizons of reason, the Spirit of Christ is manifested in a range of special gifts to inspire in the believer a receptivity to what is given from beyond the horizons of the reason-structured world. The gifts of the Spirit are thus one aspect of the resurrection effect as it affects faith and "sees" and acts in the light of what has occurred.

[41] *STh* 1–2, q. 68, a. 2.

4. Toward a Phenomenology of Revelation

I have been suggesting up to this point that the faith informing Christian consciousness does in fact possess a strong visual and contemplative character. The immediacy of the original visionary experiences of privileged witnesses need not be understood as ruling out a range of mediated modes of seeing within the living, historical community of faith—and so to allow a multidimensional evidence on the part of the faithful. In effect, we may assume that, first, the New Testament itself documents a continuing dialectic between seeing and non-seeing; and, second, that such a dialectic resists any theoretical solution. Given the possibility of mediated kinds of Christ's self-manifestation, the "seeing/non-seeing" polarity in the history of Christian experience can move us toward a more integrated self-appropriation of the life of faith. It is helpful, then, in addressing these problems, to regard the visible and invisible aspects of the New Testament account of faith to be not so much contraries, but converging perspectives. They point beyond themselves to a resolution on another plane, namely, that of the self-giving presence of the risen Jesus in the ecclesial, sacramental life of faith.

Anything resembling a systematic synthesis of what is involved in the seeing and non-seeing of faith, of the revealing and "re-veiling" of what is given, remains inevitably elusive. The complexity of the biblical and historical data on what is seen and not seen, of what appears and what has been given, and what is present and absent awaiting final disclosure, provokes a more thoroughgoing attention to the phenomenon of revelation—as explored by recent writers.[42] Clearly, idealist, subjectivist, or empiricist methods must have difficulty with the singular phenomenon of any self-revelation of a transcendent Other. Nonetheless, with some theological abandon, Jean-Luc Marion, eminent among French phenomenologists, focuses on Christ as the phenomenon saturating the whole of the New Testament and

---

[42] See Jean-Yves Lacoste, *La Phénoménalité de Dieu: Neuf études* (Paris: Cerf, 2008), 134. In a more general philosophical mode, see Anthony J. Steinbock, *Phenomenology and Mysticism: The Verticality of Religious Experience* (Bloomington and Indianapolis: Indiana University Press, 2009), 1–27. For a critical analysis of Marion's approach, see Shane Mackinlay, *Interpreting Excess: Jean Luc Marion, Saturated Phenomena, and Hermeneutics* (New York: Fordham University Press, 2010), 178–216; for a theological application, Kelly, *The Resurrection Effect*, 29–32, 44–60.

Christian life,[43] such that any consideration of either "the eyes" of faith or its "non-seeing" must be set in a much larger context.

Theology can be only enriched by a more phenomenological attentiveness, as we have suggested in an earlier chapter.[44] In its turn, theology is able to extend the range of phenomenology to the singularity of positive revelation.[45]

Still, the general phenomenological attitude remains. The phenomenon shows itself by giving itself in its overbrimming significance—and this is at its most intense and overwhelming in the case of faith's register of the gift, the giver, and the giving, from beyond all mundane perspectives.[46] But there is no implication of the phenomenon of revelation so overwhelming the recipient so as to incapacitate the subject's ability to receive and react to it. Rather, by undermining all *apriori* mindsets, the revelatory phenomenon allows the new to come into consciousness. This receptivity does not provoke a response of a purely intellectual kind, isolated from those reasons of the heart that reason itself cannot know. A purely intellectual response would be cut off from the love that recognizes no limits as it "bears all things, hopes all things, endures all things" (1 Cor 13:7-8).

For the revealed Word is given in a way that exceeds all expectations. The density and expansiveness of the Christ Event displayed in the resurrection and ascension of the crucified outstrips quantitative assessment of any kind—the neat division between seeing and non-seeing, to take one example. Moreover, there is a qualitative intensity inherent in the Christ Event that makes it "unbearable" (John 16:12), and causes it to be a troubling irruption.[47] The polarities of presence and absence, possession and dispossession, cannot but be

---

[43] Jean-Luc Marion, *Being Given: Toward a Phenomenology of Givenness*, Cultural Memory in the Present (Stanford, CA: Stanford University Press, 2002), 236.

[44] For a critical appreciation of Marion's contribution, see Brian Robinette, "A Gift to Theology? Jean-Luc Marion's 'Saturated Phenomenon' in Christological Perspective," *Heythrop Journal* 48, no. 1 (January 2007): 86–108.

[45] Jean-Luc Marion, "Le possible et la révélation," in *Eros and Eris : Contribution to a Hermeneutical Phenomenology: Liber Amicorum for Adriann Peperzak*, ed. P. van Tongeren, P. Sars, C. Bremmer and K. Boey (Dordrecht: Kluwer Academic, 1992), 217–31; *Being Given*, 216–17, 234–42, 264–68, 289.

[46] Marion, *Being Given*, 367.

[47] Ibid., 238.

kept in play. The whole frame of previous fixed points of reference and relationship is radically rearranged: the Word becomes flesh, and in that flesh, he lives, is crucified, is raised from the dead, appears to chosen witnesses, and reveals himself through multiple channels of mediation—sacramental, scriptural, preaching, and witness—in the life of the church.[48] A plurality of horizons converge and fuse in the inexhaustible excess defying all human expressions of the event (John 21:25). The singularity of Christ's appearances, of his transformed existence and continuing presence to faith, overflows the expressive range of all the terms, genres, symbols, concepts, testimonies, and descriptions related to time and place and form.[49] Thus a living communal sense of the God-given gift is the milieu in which God's primordial self-disclosure is appreciated as "Christian revelation."

Coming to faith is to come to oneself in a consciousness made new only through the self-giving Other, through a gift and a giving beyond the limits of this world (John 14:27a). This phenomenon of divine self-revelation is presented to faith, not simply to theoretic understanding. The excess of the given leaves the believer tongue-tied. As Marion remarks, because intelligence is at a loss to frame what has been received in faith into any conceptual system, it is in a sense dazzled and rendered sightless:

> Standing before Christ in glory, in agony or resurrected, it is always words (and therefore concepts) that we lack in order to say what we see, in short to see that with which intuition floods our eyes . . . God does not measure out his intuitive manifestation stingily, as though he wanted to mask himself at the moment of showing himself. But we, we do not offer concepts capable of handling a gift without measure and, overwhelmed, dazzled, and submerged by his glory, we know longer see anything.[50]

Marion is making his point, namely, the profusion and overbrimming excess of God's self-disclosure. However, the event of revelation in the face and in the flesh of the risen One does not stun or disable

---

[48] Ibid., 239.
[49] Ibid., 240.
[50] Jean-Luc Marion, "They Recognised Him, and He Became Invisible to Them," *Modern Theology* 18 (2002): 148.

contemplative intelligence and its accompanying powers of imagination. Insights, judgments, artistic expression and verbal forms,
however limited in their respective contexts, can positively nourish
and direct the contemplation of faith. The imperative remains to
allow the Christian phenomenon to disclose itself in its own evidence
and on its own terms. For Christ is encountered as the revelation
of a love and the source of life, seen and unseen, at once within the
world and beyond it. The excess of light overbrims the capacities
of meaning.[51] There is no historical end to the play of appearance
and disappearance, of presence and absence, of the seeing of chosen
witnesses and the not-seeing of those whose only light is faith itself
and the testimony of the Spirit—together with the humble creative
ministry of those who extend the Christian imagination toward what
no eye has seen, nor ear heard, nor the human heart conceived.

Conclusion

Traditional positions and their more recent transpositions indicate an understanding of what "the eyes of faith" might entail. Faith
has its senses, its hearing, its taste, its touch and its feel—something
similar to that "tact" which Coleridge understood to be the special
gift of the poet:

> He may not have it in logical coherence, in his Brain &
> Tongue; but he must have it by *Tact*: for all sounds and forms
> of Nature he must have the *ear* of a wild Arab listening in
> the silent Desert—the *eye* of a North American Indian trac-
> ing the footsteps of an Enemy upon the Leaves that strew
> the Forest; the *Touch* of a Blind Man feeling the face of a
> darling Child.[52]

We might say that this "tact" gives a holographic sense of the
realities that have been revealed. Faith is not forever fabricating a
collage of visual images drawn from mundane experience. It lives
under the gaze of the ascended Christ whose light affects Christian
experience in all its modes of seeing, hearing, and touching of "what
was from the beginning" (see 1 John 1:1-4).

---

[51] Ibid., 149.

[52] Letter to William Sotheby, in *Collected Letters of Samuel Taylor Coleridge*,
1–4, ed. E. L. Griggs, vol. 2 (Oxford, UK: Oxford University Press, 1956–71), 810.

Luke presents another perspective. On the one hand, when the crucified and risen One departs, ascending as a divine "cloud took him out of their sight" (Acts 1:9), the previous time of a particular "seeing" is over. The appearances of Jesus to his privileged disciples now yield to faith's recognition of him in every time and place. Jesus is no longer visible to human eyes, either in the mode of his earthly life, or in the privileged economy of seeing that followed on his resurrection. His ascension metaphorically depicts the accomplishment of his earthly mission through his return to the Father. On the other hand, he is now to be found in another field of perception formed by the witness of the Spirit and the continuous recollection of the whole Christ Event it inspires. The perception of faith brings its own kind of vision and wisdom. It enables faith to contemplate Christ, not in his human form within the created world, but as the one in whom all creation finds its coherence, destiny, and fulfillment (Col 1:15-20; Eph 4:10). Christ is risen, but not so as to be a visible object within the world. It is more a matter of seeing and sensing the world and its history as being taken up into the risen Christ in eschatological anticipation of what is to come. Paul's words to the Colossians awaken Christian experience to its full proportions:

> So if you have been raised with Christ, seek the things that are above, where Christ is seated at the right hand of God. Set you minds on the things that are above, not on things that are on the earth, for you have died, and your life is hidden with Christ in God. When Christ who is your life is revealed, then you also will be revealed with him in glory. (Col 3:1-4)

There is, then, a "seeking" for what is not yet possessed, and the "hidden" quality of what is not yet revealed. This "not yet" suggests a tension between what is "above" and the mundane reality "of earth." Christian consciousness ("your minds") is elevated to what is above, and orientated to what is yet to be revealed. This uplifting and future-directed experience affects the values that faith lives by, and reaches into the deepest sense of identity—"the new self, which is being renewed in knowledge according to the image of its creator" (Col 3:10), to be clothed with "compassion, kindness, humility, meekness, and patience" (Col 3:12), in a "love the binds everything together" (Col 3:14). What is implied is a distinctive form of wisdom born of being indwelt by the "word of Christ" (Col 3:16).

The experience of privileged eyewitnesses is, then, deeply formative of the tradition of faith in which "seeing" (John 14:19; 1 John
1:1-3), "non-seeing" (John 20:29) and only obscure seeing (1 Cor
13:12) are irreducible aspects. Yet that initial seeing on the part of the
eyewitnesses is a determining element in later seeing and non-seeing
of the church. Paul's "last of all" seeing bridges the gap between the
original visionary experience and the contemplative vision of faith in
later ages in the liturgical images and symbols, the art and the icons,
the sacraments as visible signs of invisible grace—and even the rare
visions that may be vouchsafed to the saintly few. All this is to say
with Augustine, *Habet namque fides oculos suos*—"For faith has
eyes of its own."[53] There is a corporate history of faith's unfolding
which receives with due reverence the witness of an original seeing
and profits from the immediacy of such a gift—as in the Browning
poem: "How will it be when none more saith 'I saw'"?[54] The fact that
some saw enables believers to move more surely in the darkness and
limitation of the life of faith now and to receive its gifts.

[53] Augustine, *Epist* 120.2.8 [PL 33:458].
[54] "A Death in the Desert" by Robert Browning, accessed October 29, 2013, www
.poetryfoundation.org/poem/173008.

Chapter 7

Theology in the Light of the Ascension

We come now to a more comprehensive theological statement, summarizing and building on the previous chapters. Admittedly, no rounded synthesis must be expected, since the very point of the ascension is that Christ has gone beyond the world of our orderly explanations. The ascension has its revelatory impact by drawing the believing mind and heart into another realm—never to be clarified until the Lord returns in glory.

Despite the inevitable tentativeness, or better, "open-endedness" of any theology of the ascension, it is worth reemphasizing that of all the events, words, and actions involved in the mystery of Jesus Christ, the ascension is closest to contemporary believers. Faith in Christ is believing in him *here and now*—in the *here* of this place, in the *now* of this time. In the concrete actuality of Christian existence, the ascended and glorified Christ is faith's point of departure. In the spontaneous intuition of faith, supported by the yearly progress of the liturgical cycle through all its feasts and seasons, the time of the ascension opens up a horizon in which all that is past, present, and still to come is integrated in terms of the one Christ Event. The whole reality of the person, life, mission, death, and resurrection of Jesus Christ can be contemplated in the various episodes of the gospel narrative or in the person-to-person intimacy of faith in the presence of Christ. Thus, the whole "mystery of Christ" is received as present, as a whole or under some particular aspect, within the experience of the living faith of the church.

Paradoxically, then, the effect of the ascension is not to disembody, dehumanize, or remove Christ. On the contrary, the ascension means that he is now present in the fullness of his humanity. In other

131

words, the ascension does not make an otherworldly abstraction of Jesus Christ. Quite the opposite: because of his ascension, the whole concreteness of his life and mission, along with the mysteries of his life and death, come together within the divine universal act of transformation. Every aspect of the mystery of Christ stands forth within the consciousness of faith in its universal relevance. Such an awareness is fundamental to the composition of the gospels and to the celebration of the liturgical year. It is also presumed, even if seldom articulated, in Christian contemplation of the various "mysteries" of Christ as, for instance, they are listed in the decades of the rosary.

Accordingly, we need constantly to emphasize that the Christ Event, in all phases and components, is, in terms of the divine intention, not only compact, but coherent and irreversible. But it is only in the light of the resurrection and the ascension that the narrative of the life, preaching, and death of Jesus be can be understood and pondered in its totality. Unless backlit by such a radiance, there would be no story to tell and none worth the telling; and there would be no one in any age disposed to listen to it. If Jesus had remained under the conditions of his previous existence, if he had not ascended to the realm of grace and of God's sheer gift manifested in the sending of the Spirit, there would be no growing capacity to receive the gift of God in its fullness, nor any need for unreserved commitment of faith. But in the domain of the Spirit, Christ continues to make himself known in a new way and in a new order of existence following his return to the Father (John 14:19, 21, 23)—in view of his eventual return as the consummation of history. Faith in the ascension holds within it a sense of existence transformed and already in the process of being drawn into the divine realm (Col 3:3).

But before running too far ahead, a summary of our investigation so far may be helpful to keep in mind the shape of a theology of the ascension as it emerges from what has gone before, and so possess a sketch or outline of what needs to be filled in as we move on. From there we can proceed to reflect more exactly on the limits and possibilities of such a theology in a way that raises questions dealing with the time and place of the ascension, its place in the revelation of mystery of Christ, and the nature of the heaven into which he has ascended.

1. A Summary So Far

First of all, then, I will make a few remarks on each chapter so far and the issues that arise. The very title of our first chapter, "Jesus Ascends—Leaving a World of Questions" matter-of-factly recognizes that the article of the Creed that speaks of Jesus rising from the dead on the third day, ascending to heaven and being seated at the right hand of the Father, and so on, stirs up a nest of difficult questions. They can be evaded or deferred, but that means giving free reign to an uncritical, figurative way of thinking that does little good. It can happen that the ascension of Christ begins to look just like a capricious projection of the human future onto another world—or, with less ambition, like a superior instance of levitation of only gravity-defying significance. It is crucial therefore to keep reflection on the ascension grounded in the biblical data and liturgical experience. For that reason, we devoted the second chapter to the variety of ways in which images, symbols, and narratives of the ascension shaped the horizon of New Testament faith and hope.

We must admit, however, that it is not sufficient simply to gather a list of texts in the New Testament that explicitly refer to the ascension. Nor is it sufficient to implicitly assume the ascension when confessing Christ's present relationship to the church and the cosmos. While such an exercise is necessary to uncover the rich and varied range of scriptural data on the ascension, it could still be too narrow a perspective. There is, after all, a larger horizon opening out from the resurrection and ascension of Christ in which all the New Testament writings are connected in a dynamic field of meaning and significance. There is a tinge of paradox here: the meaning of the ascension is not so much to be found in this or that scriptural passage in the New Testament, but rather, the whole meaning of the New Testament is to be found within the ascension, as it were, as the horizon in which the whole can be contemplated. Such is the point where Jesus receives the name that is above every name, and all creation confesses him as Lord to the glory of the Father (Phil 2:9-11).

Granting the variety and richness of the biblical data, the next step was to ground the classic biblical expressions of the ascension in a theologically attuned phenomenology, hence the third chapter, "The Phenomenon of the Ascension: Recollecting the Experience." An appreciation of the biblical data on the ascension, and attention to the singular, historic, cosmic, and eschatological sweep of its inexhaustible significance, raise the question: What was the kind of experience from which the inspired writings emerged? Theology, in dealing with the singularity of the ascension—and of every event constituting the mystery of Christ—is constantly frustrated if it is looking for a neat synthesis of what arises out of the divine initiative.

Theological exploration must remain in touch with a critically refined and flexible recollection of the experience of faith. It needs to allow for the full play of interweaving connections between the ascension and every aspect of God's self-revelation in Christ. At the same time, a deft theological phenomenology will protect this aspect of the mystery of Christ from association with mundane phenomena of a reductively physical type such as levitation, space travel, and the location of heaven beyond the stars. In short, the God-wrought event of the ascension must be allowed to appear in its own right. Receptivity to the presence of Christ, risen and ascended, demands attentiveness to what is being conveyed to the consciousness of faith, and to the manner in which it is conveyed through the words of Scripture and the biblical images.

At this point more complex issues emerge, especially those dealing with the incarnation and the ascension—or more concretely, with the body of the ascended Christ (chap. 4). The key point is this: in the light of the ascension, the incarnation is not limited to the past alone, but is an expansive and inclusive event, given the inexhaustible and incalculable extent of God's design for the salvation of the world. In other words, not only is the ascended Christ still incarnate, but we ourselves, as Christian believers, are already members of the Body of Christ. As such, we participate even now in the great transformation that has taken place in the resurrection and ascension of the crucified One. It is important to emphasize that the reality of the Body of Christ is not to be reduced to a vague sense of a metaphorical or symbolic "mystical body." Something more vital, more material, and specifically incarnational is involved. In this regard, the gift of the Spirit is not a substitute for the abiding reality of the incarnation. Rather, the Spirit is the agent of the whole expansive event of the Word made flesh (see John 16:7, 12-15). Consequently, there is a sense of time, space, and relationship that is intrinsic to the Body of Christ; and this inspires Christian confidence to resist conceptions of reality biased in a nontheological or even anti-Christian manner. Catholic faith is definitely committed to the assumption of Mary, and thereby poses a question: how is the ascension of Christ related to the assumption of Mary into heaven? More specifically, what does this Catholic Marian doctrine contribute to a fuller understanding of the ascension?

Furthermore, the expanding event of the incarnation in no way diminishes the dialogue between faith and science, but rather serves to make such exchanges more open and imaginative. Indeed, a renewed appreciation of the reality of the unfolding mystery of the Body of Christ in an "ascensional" perspective can have a twofold good effect. The "soul-less body" of materialistic modernity comes up against the transformed materiality and vitality of the cosmic Body of Christ. On the other hand, the "disembodied soul" of a rootless postmodernity meets the body-affirming reality which puts the soul back into its body—in this case, into the Body of Christ in all its relationships.

Our study comes more sharply into focus with the fifth chapter, "The Ascension and the Eucharist." It considers the usually neglected interrelationship between the ascension and the Eucharist. That connection may not seem obvious—in fact, it may seem all but contradictory. After all, the Eucharist celebrates the "real presence" of Jesus, while the ascension recognizes his present absence and inaccessibility compared to the time of his earthly life. Precisely at this point, however, distortions can creep in if no connection is made between the eucharistic Real Presence and the ascended Christ. In fact, belief in the ascension means that there is a legitimately recognized aspect of "real absence" of Christ which is quite compatible with confessing his real presence. Neither the church nor the Eucharist "contains" Christ, for it is he who is the One in whom all things are contained and are held together (Col 1:17). It is only in the wake of Christ's ascension that the Eucharist is the sacrament that it is. Christ does not ascend into the Eucharist, but the Eucharist communicates his presence because of his ascension. This is so because Christ "fills all things" (Eph 4:10), and all creation is subject to him. The earthly elements of bread and wine can be drawn into the new creation by being transformed, through the power of the Spirit, into his Body and Blood for the sustenance of the church.

Even though the Eucharist and the ascension can and must be connected, any effort in that direction leaves some further questions unanswered in the larger domain of faith's experience. Hence, a sixth chapter, "The Ascension: Out of Sight, and the Eyes of Faith," considered a dimension of the presence and absence of Christ in that he is no longer visible as he once was. There is nonetheless a sense in which the ascended One reveals himself so as to become newly visible even in the present regime of faith. Though the disciples are bidden not to look upward for the disappearing Jesus, that need not imply that they are deprived of all vision, or that faith ever afterward is blind. Augustine considered that "faith has eyes of its own." How might such a statement be understood? Christ is risen, certainly, but not so as to be a visible object within the world. The consciousness of faith is more a matter of seeing and sensing the world and its history "in Christ." The universe in its totality is taken up into the ascended Christ in eschatological anticipation of what is to come.

And so, this present chapter offers a summary of the various converging perspectives, and, we would hope, moves towards a theology of the ascension. The summary just offered cannot but provoke further inquiry, especially regarding the manner in which past, present, and future are interrelated in the one divine economy. As we move on, we pause first of all to acknowledge the limitations that theology must face.

2. Theology: Limitations and Possibilities

Having already noted the resources of tradition,[1] we can pause briefly on Aquinas's medieval exposition of the ascension. It moves over a fertile middle ground stretching between biblical figurative language and systematic theological analysis to argue that the ascension is "the cause of our salvation."[2] There are two ways in which this can be considered. The first is what today we might describe in intentional terms as Christian consciousness, for the ascension inspires the development of the theological virtues of faith, hope, and charity in response to Christ drawing his followers upwards to himself. In this regard, he is no longer thought of simply as a man on earth (see 2 Cor 5:16), but is now affirmed in the fullness of his divine-human identity.

---

[1] A good range of patristic references is presented in Kelly M. Kapic, and Wesley Vander Lugt, "The Ascension of Jesus and the Descent of the Holy Spirit in Patristic Perspective: A Theological Reading," *Evangelical Quarterly* 79, no. 1 (2007): 24–29. See also Douglas Farrow, *Ascension Theology* (London: T. &T. Clark, 2011), 18–24, 34–43; and the valuable appendices in Farrow, *Ascension and Ecclesia: On the Significance of the Doctrine of the Ascension for Ecclesiology and Christian Cosmology* (Edinburgh: T. &T. Clark, 1999), 275–98.

[2] Aquinas, *STh* III, q. 57, 6.

Secondly, the ascension causes our salvation by reason of Christ himself. By ascending, he prepares a way for his followers themselves to ascend into heaven. Since he is the head of the Body, it is fitting that the members should follow (see John 14:2-3). Moreover, he ascends as our intercessor and representative. In this role, his humanity is a kind of continuous expression of intercession (*quaedam interpellatio pro nobis*): God who exalted human nature in Christ will show mercy on those for whom the Son of God became man in the first place. Finally, by accomplishing his mission, Christ in his ascended and divine state becomes the source of gifts to all (see Eph 4:10).

Given the salvific effect of the ascension, Aquinas presumes that there is a certain movement in Christ ascending to the Father. Such change and movement cannot be excluded since he continues to possess a created human nature which cannot be ontologically unchanging and immobile. But his humanity continues in heaven;[3] and if Christ continues to be truly human, then it follows that his humanity can change (thus making possible fresh considerations of time and space already mentioned and further elaborated below). However, the change in question must be in accord with the ascended Christ's transformed state. He is no longer subject, as during his earthly life, to generation and corruption.[4] In him, humanity has entered into a new mode of existence.[5] Aquinas' conclusions here are notably relevant to a fuller theology of the ascension, as we shall see.

From the beginning of this brief study, we acknowledged that the ascension suffers from a certain theological indeterminacy. Vatican I's *Dei Filius*, plotting a middle course between agnostic and rationalist extremes, offered three possible techniques for a theological understanding of the revealed mysteries.[6] Theology can exploit, (i) *analogies* drawn from human experience; it can appeal to the (ii) *interconnection* of the mysteries of faith, and explore them for the light they shed on (iii) *the ultimate in human destiny*.

When theology addresses Christ's ascension in this way, there is a sense in which numerous *interconnections* can be made. Many

---

[3] Aquinas, *STh* III, q. 57, a. 1, ad. 1.

[4] See Aquinas, *STh* III, q. 57, a. 1.

[5] Similarly in Sergius Bulgakov, *The Lamb of God*, trans. Boris Jakim (Grand Rapids, MI: Eerdmans, 2008), 398–99.

[6] J. Neuner, and J. Dupuis, *The Christian Faith in the Doctrinal Documents of the Catholic Church* (London: Collins Liturgical Publications, 1983), n. 132, p. 45.

aspects of the Christ Event in its totality cluster around the ascension itself, namely, the resurrection of Christ from the dead, his communion with the Father, the sending of the Holy Spirit, and the presence-in-absence experience of the church and in the Eucharist, above all. Every aspect of Christ's life, death, resurrection, ascension, and return in glory continuously interconnect and interpenetrate in the one divine economy of grace and self-giving love at work in every "now." Indeed, the completion of Christ's specific mission means that he is consequently available in every moment, continuing to give himself to each generation of believers. His *kenosis*, his "self-emptying," is never exhausted. He hands over himself, his mission, his disciples, and the whole church to the economy of the Spirit.[7]

But that is not the limit of Christ's kenotic existence and action. As Paul vividly remarks, "when all things are subjected to him, then the Son himself will also be subjected to the one who put all things in subjection to him, so that God may be all in all" (1 Cor 15:28). Yet even though he is given "the name that is above every name," and though all knees should bend and every tongue confess that he is Lord"(Phil 2:9-11), his whole heavenly existence is for "the glory of the Father" and for the fulfillment of the God's saving will. Clearly, then, the technique of interconnections is particularly fruitful in the present context.

Theological exploration of the ascension in terms of its connection with "our last end," the ultimate in human destiny, and so forth, is similarly productive. It finds expression most concretely in Christ's promise to return in glory at the end of time. In a classical expression of this connection, there are the words of Jesus in John's gospel,

> In my Father's house there are many dwelling places. If it were not so, would I have told you that I go to prepare a place for you? And if I go and prepare a place for you, I will come again and take you to myself, so that where I am, there you may be also. (John 14:2-4)

But faith must move beyond itself in hope and in the longing of love if Christians are to be released into the fullest dimensions of

---

[7] Hans Urs von Balthasar, *Theo-drama: Theological Dramatic Theory*, vol. 3: *Dramatis Personae: Persons in Christ*, trans. Graham Harison (San Francisco: Ignatius Press, 1992), 520–23.

receptivity to the gift of God in Christ. The "theological virtues" need to be properly theological, and therefore attuned to the incalculable action of the Spirit, to the inexpressible mystery of the Father, and to the transformation of humanity that has occurred in the risen and ascended Christ. Otherwise, the life of faith could become fixated on "seeing" and holding onto Jesus in his previous mode of accessibility (see John 20:17). Such an attitude would fail to recognize the universal and enduring scope of what God was bringing about in Christ and the Spirit.

Clearly, these two theological possibilities—interconnecting the mysteries of faith and connecting them all to our "last end"—are valuable in our present exploration, even if the ascension is in effect a somewhat marginal consideration in a theology striving for cultural, political, and even economic relevance. That would account to some extent for the anemic character of theological speculation in this area, and why it is not a concern for a red-blooded commitment to relevance. But there is an even bigger problem. Theological development usually takes place by exploiting analogies with what is more accessible in terms of human experience. But that is the problem. Analogies appear to be lacking when it comes to exploring the meaning of the ascension. Quite simply, there are no analogies to be drawn from human experience or "things naturally known." The more these are sought, the more theological understanding seems to be clouded with a swarm of metaphors and mythological expressions—even with the projections of human fantasy. The impression could be given, as we already pointed out, that the ascension as the culmination of the mystery of Christ was merely a gravity-defying event, a superior levitation of some kind! Admittedly, in this present work, I have risked some metaphorical expressions such as "updraft," "rupture," "irruption" and so forth. But such expressions are merely evocative, designed to suggest something about how the phenomenon of the ascension of Jesus was experienced. Though there may be no appropriate analogy, there is the phenomenality of the event to be attended to and described as was attempted in chapter 2.

Admitting the lack of analogical resources is not necessarily a counsel of despair. As we saw in the chapter on the ascended body of Christ, there is an analogy deriving from the incarnation itself when this is considered as an expanding event and expressed in terms of the Body of Christ. It is illuminated in some measure by the intimate experience of our own bodily existence which inspires analogical reflection on the expanding event of the incarnation. In this analogy, "my body" is not merely a physical object which I "have" or possess. It is rather the vibrant network of relationships in which I exist in the world. In this perspective, the body is a "given" in the immediate experience of each personal subject. It is not, however, an individual organism enclosed in its own skin, but the matrix of manifold and interrelated dimensions of embodiment found in relation to other human beings, to all living things, and to the earth, the land, time, space, and nature. The body language of the New Testament stretches to differing kinds of corporeal relationships—the sexual, maternal, familial, social, ecological, cosmic. All of these can throw light on the eschatological but expanding reality of the Body of Christ (Eph 4:4). These bodily connections presuppose the worldly, material, social, and generative character of human existence. Analogically related to the Body of Christ, such bodily features serve to disclose the love and generativity of Christ in relation to the church. It follows that sacraments are the actions of Christ (Eph 4:10) within history configuring the church little by little to himself.

The original mode of the incarnation as it was embodied in the birth, life, suffering, and death of Jesus of Nazareth was inevitably categorized in temporal, spatial, and cultural limitations. But when the trajectory of the incarnational event comes to a universalization in the ascension, the dimensions of incarnation manifest God's plan that Christ fill all things (Eph 4:10, cf. 1:23). A new incarnational reality grows to its generative maturity in that interpenetration of the world and heaven in the time of the church (Eph 5:21-32). The Body of Christ understood in this way assumes that there is a new mode of corporeality, with its own distinctive mode of knowing and sensibility. Mind and heart are affected by personal participation in the vertical and horizontal expansion of the incarnation. The scale includes the vertical since it arises only from the gift of God, from "on high," unconditioned by any human condition. But horizontal also, since there is room for formulating knowledge, educating sensibilities, and shaping commitments within the experience of the church in the world.

By exploiting this analogy of the embodied experience, we are led to fresh considerations of the Body of Christ. He incorporates his followers into his Body throughout history and through the church—and above all through the Eucharist, which is uniquely Christ's bodily self-giving within and for the church. In the Body of

Christ, the natural dimensions of bodily being are transformed and become freshly perceived when set against the horizon illumined by Christ's resurrection and ascension.

Christ's bodily transformation must include nature itself—for in the nature of the new creation, death is no more, the dead are raised in Christ, and life is ultimately fulfilled in the face-to-face vision of God. A new cosmic and theocentric order comes into being in Christ. Its field of generative relationships constitutes a new nature, a new principle of action, anticipated in the church's celebration of the Eucharist. In the ascended Jesus, time, space, body, and nature are refashioned, and history, instead of being a concatenation of episodic events, is caught up in the updraft of all things being gathered into Christ. With the coming of the Spirit, the trinitarian outreach into creation is fulfilled; and a new phase of ingathering begins, terminating only when both Christ and Spirit present all creation to the Father, and God is "all in all" (1 Cor 15:28).

3. Time after the Ascension

The ascension is both a movement and a horizon, suggested in the words of Jesus, "I go to prepare a place for you" (John 14:2) in his Father's house of many rooms. He goes on to assure his disciples, "And if I go and prepare a place for you, I will come again and take you to myself, so that where I am, you may be also" (John 14:3).[8] The ascension therefore is not a mythological addition to the paschal mystery, but the movement and horizon in which God's ingathering action is occurring. From that point of view, Christ's ascension and departure from this world amounts to the making of the Christian heaven. For Jesus ascends, not simply in his individual humanity, but as embodying a world perfected, transformed, and offered to the Father—diaphanous with the Light (Rev 21:23). According to the explicit promise of Jesus to Nathanael—here representing all future disciples—"You will see the heaven opened, and the angels of God ascending and descending on the Son of Man" (John1:51). The hitherto "closed heaven" is now opened in such a way that the glorified Son of Man is the new channel of communication between God and creation. Jesus will be the new Jacob's ladder (Gen 28:12-17),

---

[8] See Farrow, *Ascension and Ecclesia*, 263–64; and Hans Urs von Balthasar, *Man in History: A Theological Study* (London: Sheed and Ward, 1972), 287–88.

connecting what is above with what is below, what is at the center and what at the circumference of existence (see John 3:13).

And so the ascended Jesus is the realization of a new communication between God and the world. Because he who is most intimate to the Father became accessible in the flesh of this world, believers can now find their way to the Father and to a dwelling in his house (John 14:1-4).[9] The ascended Christ is constituted as "being for" the world, ever active in his eucharistic self-giving and breathing forth his Spirit.

Yet here the most difficult questions arise. The compact paschal event of Jesus' death, burial, resurrection, and glorification unfolds over the course of time, and is revealed in time.[10] There are implications for how the new creation as "time in Christ" is lived and understood. There is no suggestion of a seamless insertion of God's transcendent action on behalf of the crucified Son into an untroubled flow of events. A singularity has occurred: the crucified One has been raised up, and this is the beginning of the new creation. The old world of time and space is not left undisturbed. In this new creation, Jesus does not become disembodied or disincarnate. Consequently, he is not rendered timelessly static. It is not as though nothing more happens for him, or, at the other extreme, that time has no goal and dissipates meaninglessly in an endless flow of discrete moments. It is better, then, to imagine the ascended Jesus inaugurating "the fullness of time." In what and who he is, he brings time to its fullness, gathering the scattered moments of undecided time into a flow directed to the glory of the Father. Within this new time, the Body of Christ grows toward that ultimate point when "God will be all in all" (1 Cor 15:27).

In regard to the Body of Christ, we are justified in speaking of a *process* of glorification. However, that does not mean that each moment of the process has no value in itself, nor that, in part or in whole, it is producing the glory of Jesus. Christ is not in time as subject to it, but rather, the whole flow of time is subject to him: "Jesus

---

[9] Anthony J. Kelly and Francis J. Moloney, *Experiencing God in the Gospel of John* (Mahwah, NJ: Paulist Press, 2003), 287–89, and von Balthasar, *Theo-Drama: Theological Dramatic Theory*, vol. 5, *The Last Act*, trans. Graham Harison (San Francisco: Ignatius Press, 1998), 376–79.

[10] See Lohfink, *Die Himmelfahrt Jesu: Untersuchungen zu die Himmelfahrts-und Erhohungstexten bei Lukas*, Studien zum Alten und Neuen Testament 26 (Munich: Kösel-Verlag, 1971), especially 279–81.

Christ is the same yesterday and today and forever" (Heb 13:8). Indeed, the incarnation as it expands in the resurrection-ascension initiates a new form of temporality. Christ has time and makes space for his followers in a new way.[11] Von Balthasar suggests that the time of the forty days prefigures that aspect of the time of the church in which Christ is encountered in the sacraments and in other ways.[12] Christ's ascension is an ending of a previous mode of life, as he vanishes from the visibilities of earthly existence. That invisibility makes quite clear that the church does not possess, control, or contain Christ. Rather, that totality is contained by him. Christ is not "in" the sacraments, just as he is not "in" the world. Rather, elements of the world—the bread and wine, oil, water, and so on—are, through the action of the Spirit, assumed "into Christ," transfigured by him as anticipations of the new creation—so to become the sacraments of faith. The sacramental economy, being permanent, is guaranteed in the efficacy of its communication of the grace of Christ's presence. This is different from the episodic and privileged appearances of the risen Christ over the forty-day period. The time of the sacraments has no end as long as history continues.

In short, Christ is the fullness of time. He is not subject to its fragmentation but freely gathers what was, what is, and what is to come, into this incarnate being. In the light of the ever-expanding event of the incarnation, history takes on an eschatological density. Through the ascension Christ rises above history, but not as a flight from it. Rather, that history has a new density and direction. Under the guidance of the Spirit, it is made to serve our embodied coexistence in Christ, as the incarnation event expands from one generation to the next. Time no longer has the power to delay the realization of our true selves in him, nor to fragment and undermine our deepest relationship to the world. And yet, the time of Christ is the time of eschatological surprises. It is not simply biological time (with its aging and entropy), but the time of an ever broader and deeper realization of our true selves in the Body of Christ. Time in Christ has entered into the trinitarian eternity of loving exchange. Its flow and direction remains so that the interpersonal communion existing between the Father and the Son can be extended to all ages, from one generation to the next (John 17:20-24).

[11] See Hans Urs von Balthasar, *A Theology of History* (London: Sheed and Ward, 1963), 23–77.
[12] Ibid., 87.

All this is to say that the ascension does not take Christ out of time, but is the condition for his complete immersion in it, as its fullness. Faith is the consciousness of having time "in him," so that he becomes the measure and goal of time. If time is "the measure of motion," the Body of Christ is the fullest measure of what is truly moving in history and in the universe itself—gifts are poured out "for the building up of the body of Christ until all of us come to the unity of faith and of the knowledge of the Son of God, to maturity, to the measure of the full stature of Christ" (Eph 4:12-13). Jesus, in his ascent to the Father, brings time to its redemptive completion.

It follows that the time of the church must keep finding a fresh focus in the ascension. With that focus comes a sense of proportion arising from the dialectic of presence and absence. Without it, there can be a loss of eschatological realism and the presence of Christ can tend to be interpreted as a presence of one object in a world of other objects. As a result, awareness of his unique mode of presence as the anticipation of the eschatological realization of all things in him is diminished. Moreover, unless the eschatological character of the presence of Christ is acknowledged, there is the danger of absolutizing the church as the Body of Christ as a purely historical or social entity. The radical analogy of the Body of Christ is compromised by any univocal tendency to reduce it to a merely earthly embodiment in terms, say, of social network or political solidarity.[13] In this era of time after the ascension when the church believes without seeing, Christ is more perfectly present in each "now" than could ever have been the case in his earthly life.

4. From Experience to Meaning

Our reflection has been moving from the experience of the ascension—biblically and phenomenologically "recollected"—to its theological meaning, from receptivity to the phenomenon to thinking about its significance. We have already mentioned that the ascension pervades the New Testament in different ways and in different contexts (cf. Luke 24:50-53; Acts 2:30-35; John 20:17; Mark 16:19; Eph 4:8-10; 1 Tim 3:16; Heb 4:14; 9:27). The phenomenon can be viewed from varying perspectives so as to suggest a dialectic of presence and absence, seeing and non-seeing, that can never be resolved

---

[13] See Farrow, *Ascension Theology*, 51–63.

on this side of the Parousia. Furthermore, belief in the ascension is an uncontested article of faith in the Creed. It fits into a particular sequence largely determined by the Luke-Acts periodization of the paschal event as it culminates in the ascension. The ascension is the point from which Luke "looks back" over the whole life and mission of Jesus; and from which, he "looks forward" into the life and mission of the church. The retrospective view entails the recognition of Christ as the individual Jesus of Nazareth. The prospective view recognizes the living, present reality of the crucified and risen Jesus as the Christ—and the fulfillment that is promised. More precisely, the history of Christian consciousness contains a recollection of both an economy of post-resurrection appearances of Jesus, and their ending (1 Cor 15:3-11). But this ending leads into the time of his ascension, in which Jesus lives as the conqueror of death, and as embodying the new creation which will be fully realized with his return at the end of history.

The event of Christ's ascension is, however, resistant to precise description and definition. It is best known through its effects—by the way it resonates in the lived experience of the church, its symbols, and the narratives that form the horizon of Christian faith, with its retrospective and prospective dimensions. Heavenly figures discourage the efforts of the disciples to scan the skies, to peer into the realm of the transcendent God, or to project calculations from the world below. On the other hand, there is a certain participation "from above," in that faith and hope share in the mind of the ascended One (see Col 3:2-3). There opens a downward perspective of sharing in the mind of the glorified Son, this Jesus who, acclaimed as Lord, has received the "name above all names." For faith shares his vision of the world and the universe itself, moving toward its cosmic transformation. This is to anticipate the eschatological realization of the Body of Christ offered to the glory of God the Father.

The risen Christ's self-disclosures to privileged witnesses (Acts 10:41 and 1 Cor 15:4-11), come to an end. He ascends into heaven. As a result, faith is earthed in the reality of an ending, a departure, a closure—and a subsequent expansion in the time of faith and in the light of the Spirit. In this regard, there is no room for spiritual docetism that would pretend that Jesus is present as he was before. When all the episodes constitutive of divine revelation depend on God's free action, any attempt to gain a systematic overview must be modest.

There is, however, some theological intelligibility to be found in the Luke-Acts presentation. It arises from the historical need for witnesses to be formed (and, indeed, transformed) by the resurrection of the crucified. That would take time, and imply on God's part some accommodation to the disciples and their needs. Consequently, the time after the resurrection can be taken as God-given time, allowing for the reality of the resurrection to sink into the consciousness of faith and be appreciated as a world-transforming event in all its dimensions.

But this raises the question of the significance of the forty days for Christ himself, and whether it is more than an extended learning experience for the disciples. As already suggested, this period can be considered as a time of progressive glorification for Christ himself (cf. John 20:17), culminating in his sending the Spirit—and reaching its fulfillment in his return at the end of time. However such "stages" or "phases" might be conceived, they occur within the dynamics of a proto-trinitarian event of communication: Jesus ascends to the Father and to the glory that was his before the foundation of the world (John 17:5). His return to the Father marks the sending of the Spirit so that "the Spirit of truth" will guide believers "into all truth," glorifying Jesus and declaring "the things that are to come" (see John 16:13-14). Within this quasi-trinitarian economy, the past, present, and future are interrelated. The Christ Event coheres in its various phases and remains irreversible within the dynamics of the reciprocal glorification of Father, Son, and Holy Spirit. Christ, glorified by the Father and the Spirit, contains within himself all that preceded his present state when he proclaimed the kingdom of the Father—his obedience, his words, his healing gestures, the passion itself. He is the anticipation of everything that will follow from it, namely, the sending of the Holy Spirit and his return as the judge and fulfillment of human history.

5. The Heaven of the Ascension

In his ascension, Christ departs into the indefinability of the realm of God from which the Spirit, the other Paraclete, will come (John 16:7). How are these events related?[14] Theological intelligence

---

[14] See Hans Urs von Balthasar, *Theo-Logic: Theological Logical Theory*, vol. 3, *The Spirit of Truth*, trans. Graham Harison (San Francisco: Ignatius Press, 2005), 297–301, for stimulating elaboration of this point.

generally appreciates that in God's actual free dispensation of grace and mercy, the objective offer of the gift of God—the incarnation in all its mysteries—must be accompanied by the God-given capacity to receive it, namely, the gift of the Spirit (see John 16:23). If Jesus has remained under the conditions of the previous economy, if he had not ascended to the incalculable realm from which all comes as sheer gift, the receptivity and unreserved character of faith would be compromised.

The ascension of Jesus makes "heaven" the realm from which the Spirit—the gift preceding and crowning all gifts—is given. The life of the world to come is not a human production or a worldly resource, but the gift from "on high." It is an incalculable gift of the Spirit, breathing where it will (John 3:8). In the Pauline idiom, the ascension means not only that Christ fills all things, but also that he is the source of all gifts necessary for the building up of his Body (see Eph 4:7-11). As gifts abound from the realm to which Christ has ascended, so too does thanksgiving and serene longing for the promised return of Christ (cf. John 16:7; 16:24; 17:13). There is no desire to cling to the past as if faith were an endless reconfiguration of the recorded memories of Jesus of Nazareth within the dimensions of the present world (John 20:17). For Paul, the human point of view is a horizontal perspective on Jesus untroubled by the vertical disruption of his resurrection and ascension (2 Cor 5:16). Only a horizon enlarged by faith in the resurrection and ascension of Jesus can appreciate that Christ embodies "a new creation: everything old has passed away" (2 Cor 5:17).[15]

After these remarks on the time of the ascension, the related question of "where" arises. It is easier to ask than to answer. Has the body of Christ been relocated in some other realm? Admittedly, metaphors of location cannot be avoided (e.g., John 14:3). However, that does not necessitate the invention of a particular sacred space or heavenly location somehow added to the physical world of our experience. Nor does it mean the invention of some form of celestial physics. But there is another more destructive extreme when the ascension is taken to mean in effect the displacement of the physical reality of Christ, so as to mean what amounts to an "excarnation."

[15] For this section, see José Granados, "The First Fruits of the Flesh and the First Fruits of the Spirit: The Mystery of the Ascension," *Communio* 38, no. 2 (Spring 2011): 6–38.

If the Word was made flesh (John 1:14), does the present situation of Christ, ascended into heaven, suggest that his flesh, his bodily being, has been volatilized and so spiritualized that the incarnation ceases to be after his resurrection and ascension? The only possible solution is to be found in a more comprehensive theology of the incarnation so that it includes the resurrection and ascension—and indeed, the formation of the Body of Christ through time and space. This we attempted in a previous chapter. Christ, at each phase of the incarnation, remains the same person (Luke 24:39; Heb 13:8), even if the incarnation is an expanding event, as Christ draws to himself all creation.[16] When one considers the great "cosmic" christological statements of John and Paul (John 1:3-5; 1 Cor 15:25-28; Eph 1:3-10; Col 1:15-17; Heb 1:1-4; Rev 1:12-16), the overriding concern of the New Testament writers is not to locate Christ within the cosmos from which he has departed, but to view the totality of the world in its fabric and movement within the redemptive reality of Christ. He embodies the new creation, its origin, form, coherence, and goal.

Two facets of the ascension are to be kept in mind if its meaning is to be appropriately expressed. First, it is a divine act in regard to Christ, constituting him as Lord. Second, it is a divine act for the formation of the church. There will always be more to be said, especially in regard to the dialectic of presence and absence. With the ascension of Jesus into the cloud of divine glory, there will indeed be a "cloud of unknowing"—sufficient to justify the vast and varied tradition of the *via negativa*. But from out of this absence, this negation, this darkness of familiar knowledge with its fixed bearings and clear outlines, Christ will appear, as the fulfillment of all our knowing and hoping. But he does not come as an idea, but in his personal identity, indeed, as the Word incarnate *in person* and in the universal outreach of his identity.

Aquinas's approach leads into some larger considerations. For instance, it would not be extreme to propose that the resurrection and ascension of Jesus "deconstruct" the categories and language of mundane thinking and even religious expression. The holding capacity of the old wineskins becomes inadequate in regard to the fresh wine of revelation (Matt 9:16-17; Mark 2:21-22; Luke 5:36-

---

[16] See Hans Urs von Balthasar, *Theo-Drama: Theological Dramatic Theory*, vol. 5, *The Last Act*, trans. Graham Harison (San Francisco: Ignatius Press, 1998), 376–79.

39). Christ has ascended beyond this world of creation into another inexpressible realm in anticipation of God being "all in all" (1 Cor 15:27). The life of faith is now a matter of waiting for the revelation and advent of this other realm when Christ returns. Human beings may well think forward to that event and even be tempted to fill the present with an array of definite objects of shape, color, and temporal sequence in order to describe the ascension in the language and imagery of a provisional world. That temptation throws light on the strange paradox that occurs at the heart of revelation. For all the explicitness of their promise of eternal life, for the variety of images employed to that purpose, the Scriptures in fact exhibit a marked reserve in describing the realities they most witness to.

There is a triple silence in the Christian narrative. There is the dark silence of death, when the Word is silenced and Jesus is dead and buried. Then there is the luminous silence in which faith trembles before the empty tomb and witnesses to the appearances of the risen One, when faced with the utterly other and the utterly new. This is followed by the further deep silence of the Son's ascension to the Father, into the heart of the Mystery and source of all gifts and giving. The essential and singular parable of Christ's life, death, resurrection, and ascension takes none of the waiting or silence out of the hope it inspires for what no eye has seen, what no ear heard, and what no human heart has conceived regarding the fulfillment of God's promises (1 Cor 2:9). Though faith follows the ascended Christ into the universal reach of his presence, there is no assurance of clarity, and the ways of God remain beyond all human calculation (Rom 11:33). No matter how unreserved the promise of eternal life for those who believe, "it has not yet appeared what we shall be" (1 John 3:2). All that is known is that "when he is revealed, we will be like him," in the full evidence of the Light. The ascension precludes fitting the gift of God into the proportions of human calculation.

The humility of the early New Testament witnesses is evidenced in a sobering record of their naivety. Though Christ "had presented himself alive to them by many convincing proofs" (Acts 1:3), unable to get beyond their own narrow horizon, they had asked, "Lord, is this the time when you will restore the kingdom to Israel?" (Acts 1:6). Jesus' answer is instructive: "It is not for you to know the times or the periods that the Father has set by his own authority" (Acts 1:7). These disciples are then commissioned to be his witnesses "in Jerusalem, in all Judea and Samaria, and to the ends of the earth"

(Acts 1:8). The restoration of the kingdom to Israel ceases to be a pressing concern. Even the oldest recorded prayer in the New Testament, "Maranatha! Our Lord, come!" (1 Cor 16:22; Rev 22:20), so expressive of longing and hope, presupposes nothing other than the identity of Jesus—crucified, risen, and ascended, and as promising his return at the end of time. Hope certainly anticipates sharing in the glory of Christ in a bodily manner, when the "perishable . . . dishonorable . . . weak . . . physical" (1 Cor 15:35), will become in conformity to him, "imperishable, glorious, powerful, spiritual" (1 Cor 15:42-44). Belief in Christ's ascension outstrips faith's capacity to represent the future, giving way to patience and hope in him who "by the power at work within us is able to do far more abundantly than all we ask or think" (Eph 3:20).

The effect of the ascension is to discourage any attempt to reduce the future to the categories and structures of this present sphere of our experience: "hope that is seen is not hope" (Rom 8:24). Hope expands to its proper proportions only by following Christ in his ascent to the Father and awaiting his return. Even the best intentions of prayer remain subject to the inspiration of the Spirit: "for we do not know how to pray as we ought, but that very Spirit intercedes for us with sighs too deep for words" (Rom 8:26). Christian consciousness must learn to live not only with its faith in the ascension unimpeded by narrow patterns of understanding and representation of the world Christ has transcended—that is, in not clinging to him in his not-yet-ascended state (John 20:17)—but also with a certain not-willing (see Acts 1:6-7). It must yield the mundane desires latent even in our best prayers and hopes to the incalculable dimensions of the Spirit and will of the Father.

To summarize: the crucified Jesus died, was buried, and remains dead to this life and its world. Yet he has risen from the dead into another order of existence and disclosed himself alive in another realm to chosen witnesses. This mode of self-disclosure was episodic, and with the ascension of the risen One to the right hand of the Father, this privileged mode of seeing came to an end. Blessedness now consisted in believing rather than in seeing Jesus, either in terms of his previous human existence in the world, or in the mode of privileged episodic encounters after the resurrection. Indeed, the ascension of Christ in terms of the divine economy of salvation means that he is "out of sight"—in the way that God is out of sight, even though the Holy Spirit is sent and Jesus' promise to return remains.

And yet there is the sacramental presence of Christ to the church. And in the experience of Christian life, faith, though not seeing, is not blind. While there is no point in looking up to heaven, nor looking into the empty tomb, there is every reason within the consciousness of faith to look in other directions—within the corporate, sacramental, eschatological perspectives that have been opened up. There results a larger imaginative or affective manner of "seeing" what God has revealed. In the light of the ascension, the coming of the Spirit, and the promise of Jesus to return at the end of time, the manifold expressions of incarnational faith can go beyond themselves and communicate the presence of Christ, despite the essential darkness of faith: "you have not seen him and yet you love him." (1 Pet 1:8-9). In this respect, with all its symbolic retinue of metaphor and symbol, the ascension is the paradigmatic instance of imaginative expression going beyond all powers of expression, even while relying on the mediation of images (ascent, the cloud, the Father's right hand, heavenly figures, and so forth).[17] Faith follows the ascended One out of the world of experience, above the available world of representations and conceptual systems, to the unutterable reality of communion with him who will return, and who now draws the faithful into the unity existing between himself and the Father.[18] Even though a new order of existence has been inaugurated, there is a distance, a hiddenness, and a radical demand inherent in it:

> seek the things that are above where Christ is, seated at the right hand of God. Set you minds on things that are above, not on things that are on earth, for you have died and your life is hidden with Christ in God. When Christ who is your life is revealed, then you will be revealed with him in glory. (Col 3:1-4)

As Bulgakov wisely remarks, the ascension, far from being a withdrawal or diminishment in terms of God's relationship to the

---

[17] With regard to Luke's employment of the cloud symbolism, Lohfink remarks, in *Die Himmelfahrt Jesu*, "Die Wolke war bereits fur ihn ein biblisches Symbol, theologische Chiffre fur Dinge, die nur in Bild und Gleichnis anschaulich zu machen sind" (283). His fine book concludes with a quotation from Maximus of Turin: (*ibid*), citing Maximus of Turin, Sermo XLIV 3 (CChrL XXIII, 179).

[18] See Jean-Luc Nancy, *Au fond des images* (Paris: Editions Galilée, 2003).

world, shows forth the God-world relationship in a clearer light.[19] In the ascent of the glorified humanity, time and space are newly configured. Chalcedon retains its validity in heaven. The hypostatic relationship of the divine person to humanity is not lessened but expanded. The continuance and expansion of the humanity of the ascended Christ makes clear that there is no God without the world; and there is no world apart from God. To use a spatial metaphor, the world, owned, claimed, finalized in Christ, is now forever "in God." As was mentioned above, Aquinas considered that the ascension was the "cause" of salvation. In another idiom, it can be said that the ascension is not completed in the exaltation of Christ, but spills over, as it were, into the eventual ascension of all.[20] To that degree, it has the character of an unbounded event of universal effect. As Christ ascends and is glorified in his self-emptying surrender to the Father's will, his kenosis continues through all time and space. Though all things are now subject to him, he is exalted in his subjection to the Father so that "God may be all in all" (1 Cor 15:28). Although he now possesses "the name that is above every name" (Phil 2:9), and all creation exalts the name of Jesus, he exercises his universal lordship "to the glory of God the Father" (Phil 2:11).

Any theology of the ascension must appreciate what is at stake. This lies in the incalculable originality of the divine mystery. From one point of view, the ascension of Christ represents the most extravagant statement of positive theology. From another perspective, it demands a thoroughgoing negative theology, for the ascension, even though it "means the world" to Christian faith—the world possessed by God and transformed by the divine Spirit—theologically speaking, is "out of the world" in terms of any available analogies, concepts or symbols pretending to depict it. Positivity and negativity are intertwined. Each aspect impels toward the other, and both look beyond themselves to the singularity of the ascension itself. Thus, the ascension occupies a point outside all human experience, beyond the limits of death, beyond even our understanding of the resurrection-event itself, to be ultimately definable only by the mystery of God itself.

To repeat: phenomenological attentiveness is needed if what is given to the experience of faith is to be received on its own terms.

---

[19] Bulgakov, *The Lamb of God*, 317–403, especially 398–99.
[20] Ibid., 400.

What is at stake is letting in the light and atmosphere of a new creation. Just as the risen Jesus entered the locked rooms to the surprise of his fearful disciples, a more phenomenological receptivity helps create a space more responsive to the light of Christ and the fresh air of his Spirit. The conclusion of John's gospel remains a healthy reminder: the risen Jesus is not contained within the linear print of any book—or of all the books of the world (John 21:25). The phenomenon exceeds all efforts to express it.

In that respect, questions about the ascension, the Body of Christ, and materiality of creation[21] have already demanded some reference to the Catholic doctrine of the assumption of our Lady, solemnly defined in 1950. This is one more point where, theologically speaking, the intentionality of faith has hurried past its powers of expression. If Mary is declared to be assumed, body and soul, into heaven, then the corporate, historical authority of the Catholic Church is thereby committed to a view of materiality, corporeality, and physicality in a way that is largely beyond our powers of expression, in either conceptual or even imaginative terms. Here we can do little more than note that it would be of great ecumenical significance if our understandings of the ascension of Christ and the assumption of Mary interacted more positively. In the concrete liturgical unfolding of Catholic tradition, the ascension of Jesus would be deprived of its salvific significance if unrelated to the assumption of Mary as cause to effect. Likewise, the assumption, if more clearly connected to the ascension of Christ, would have a clearer ecclesiological and cosmic significance. Here we can make only a few remarks.

In both cases, faith stretches forward and upward. Ambrose of Milan expressed the cosmic sweep of the mystery of Christ with the words, "In Christ's resurrection, the world arose. In Christ's resurrection, the heavens arose; in Christ's resurrection the earth itself arose."[22] Such all-embracing declarations have influenced our present reflection on the ascension. We have emphasized the significance of the ascension as the completion and expansion of incarnation. That enables us to glimpse the connections between the incarnation, the ascension, and the universal transformation anticipated in the Catholic doctrine of Mary "assumed body and soul into heaven."

---

[21] Bulgakov, *The Lamb of God*, 393–98.
[22] *De excessu fratris sui*, bk 1. PL 16, 1354.

In such a context, the assumption of Mary is a concrete symbol of the overbrimming significance of the ascension itself. Now assumed into the glory of Christ, she is the anticipation of the heaven of a transfigured creation.[23] In that regard, Mary is the paradigmatic instance of creation open to, collaborating with, and transformed by the creative mystery of God in Christ.

As the Mother of Christ, Mary symbolizes the generativity of creation under the power of the Spirit. In her, as the Advent antiphon has it, "the earth has been opened to bud forth the Savior." In its confession of the assumption, Christian hope finds a particular confirmation. In Mary, now assumed body and soul into the heaven of God and Christ, our humanity, our world, and even our history have reached their divinely-destined term. She embodies the reality of our world as having received into itself the mystery that is to transform the universe in its entirety.

The seer of the Book of Revelation invites his readers to share the vision of "the holy city, the new Jerusalem, coming down out of heaven from God, prepared as a bride adorned for her husband" (Rev 21:1-3). Such a vision, as we have seen, is the background for both a theology of the ascension of the one who uniquely descended from on high, and of Mary's assumption as the New Eve. In Mary's assumption, our world is diaphanous to the glory of God and the great cosmic marriage begins. The Spirit has brought forth in her the particular beauty of creation as God sees it. In her, human history has come to its maturity, its age of consent, to surrender to the transcendent love for which it was destined. Out of such a union, the whole Christ of a transfigured creation is born. Thus, while the focus of Christian hope is in Christ's death, resurrection, and ascension, there is a *reprise*, as it were, of the paschal mystery in its efficacy. In the assumption of Mary into heaven, the gift of Christ's transforming grace has already been received. It has attained its transforming effect. The ascended Christ has conformed her to himself so that she embodies receptivity to the gift of God who "has raised us up with him and seated us with him in the heavenly places in Christ Jesus, so that in the ages to come he might show the immeasurable riches of his grace in kindness towards us in Christ Jesus" (Eph 2:6-7).

---

[23] See Karl Rahner, "The Interpretation of the Dogma of the Assumption," *Theological Investigations* 1, trans. C. Ernst (London: Darton, Longman and Todd, 1961), 215–27.

Assumed into the heaven of her Son's ascension, Mary is no longer subject to the rule of death (1 Cor 15:42-58). Her transformed existence is no more enclosed in the materiality of a world undisturbed by the resurrection and the ascension of the crucified One. United to Christ, Mary lives and acts, and continues to act, as the Mother of the church. In the heaven of Christ, her intercessory prayer and compassionate involvement has a measureless influence. Invoked as Mother of the church, Our Lady, Help of Christians, Mother of Mercy or Mother of Perpetual Help, Our Lady of Guadalupe (indeed, in all the invocations of the Litany of Loreto, and more), she is present in the divine realm of endless life and love. Mary of Nazareth is the name of a historical person—the mother of Jesus. Yet history has no record of her life except through the documents of faith, above all, the gospels of the New Testament.

It is significant in the present context that Mary has become known to faith only through the immense transformation that took place in the resurrection and ascension of her Son, and its impact on human consciousness through faith, hope, and love. The assumption enables faith to glimpse the "opened heaven" of Jesus' promise to the disciples in his conversation with Nathanael: "Amen, amen, I say to you, you will see heaven opened and the angels of God ascending and descending on the Son of Man" (John 1:51). Her Son embodies the open heaven of communication between God and creation. But in Mary, the effects of that communication are anticipated in a way appropriate to her vocation as Mother of the whole Christ, head and members.

In short, the salvific effect of the ascension of Christ comes home to the life of faith through the assumption of Mary—a determining feature of Catholic ecclesial experience and tradition. To avoid mentioning the assumption in this present work would leave the theology of the ascension of Christ without its more personal effect. Furthermore, if the assumption of Mary is left disconnected from the ascension of Christ, it can quickly become a devotional "optional extra," and cease to be carrier of the universal and cosmic transformation of all creation in Christ. On the other hand, in the light of the ascension, in which the presence and activity of Christ is viewed, belief in the assumption of the Mother of Christ, body and soul, into heaven cannot but continue to inspire a fresh hearing of this exhortation from the Letter to the Ephesians,

So if you have been raised with Christ, seek the things that
are above, where Christ is seated at the right hand of God.
Set your minds on the things that are above, not on things
that are on earth, for you have died, and your life is hidden
with Christ in God. When Christ who is your life is revealed,
then you will be revealed with him in glory. (Eph 3:1-4)

Conclusion

In bringing this brief sketch of a theology of the ascension to a
conclusion, we recall the converging perspectives suggested in the
previous chapters dealing with the scriptural, phenomenological,
incarnational, sacramental, and experiential aspects of the Christ
ascending to the realm of the Father.

It is clear that a theology of the ascension is not without special
challenges. The risen Christ ascends beyond the familiar world of
human experience and into the fathomless depths of God. In an obvious sense, such a theology necessarily proceeds "by way of negation"
if the believing mind is to break free from the myths and mundane
images that tend to infect common understandings of the resurrection and the ascension. And yet there is the overwhelming positivity
of expectation: the Christ who has departed this world is to return
in the fullness of his evidence. Such an expectant longing does not
leave Christian faith and its attendant mysticism merely in a zone of
always increasing negation. Whatever the distortions and deficiencies
that theology and prayer must transcend, whatever the limitations
inherent in concepts and images that must be acknowledged in order
to negate and surpass them, there is no question of renouncing the
expectation of Christ's return—however incalculable that might be.

Still, theology in the light of the ascension can inhabit the in-
between of Christ's departure and eventual return with its own
creativity. It can foster an appropriate intelligence of what God is
revealing in the ascension by making connections between its various
aspects—trinitarian, christological, pneumatological, ecclesiological,
sacramental, liturgical, mystical, and so forth. In that way, theology
can suggest a certain synthesis in its effort to say something rather
than nothing. But even that is looking to Christ's return and its
relationship to the eschatological consummation of all things in
God. The problem in all of this is that a theology of the ascension
is notably lacking in any range of analogies it can appeal to. Even

trinitarian theology can employ quite a suite of psychological and communitarian analogies to elucidate, in some way, the unity and Trinity of God. But such possibilities do not seem to be available when it comes to a theology of the ascension.

Nonetheless, two considerations seem to offer a way forward. First, by conceiving of the ascension in its relationship to the expanding event of the incarnation, we preclude the tendency to think of the ascension as his disembodiment, dehumanization, or "excarnation." The continuance and expansion of the incarnation, when so understood, has profound ecclesiological and eschatological significance. Second, not only is the incarnation conceived of as an expanding event, but the meaning of the embodiment emerges in a world and in the church—the Body of Christ. The phenomenon of existing and communicating in the body suggested a range of analogical applications to the transformed bodiliness of Christ, his embodiment in the church, and his communication to it through the sacraments, the Eucharist above all.

Because of the ascension, elemental notions such as "world," "heaven," "time," and "place" need to be recast. If Christ has ascended in his humanity into heaven, then humanity and the world in which it is inextricably immersed has entered into a new mode of existence. It is not as though Christ has left the world. He now relates to it in a new way—our humanity has not been discarded in the ascended Christ. In this sense, heaven, in Christian terms, is not a vague celestial location but communion with God in Christ in a creation transformed. It is, in the words of Jesus in John's gospel, "the opened heaven," with "the angels of God ascending and descending upon the Son of Man" (John 1:51). Through Christ's ascension to the Father, a new age of communication between God and the world is inaugurated. In Christ, the world has been irreversibly taken up into the life of God, and God has come down into the life of the world. As has been emphasized on previous occasions, it is no longer a matter of fitting Christ into an unredeemed world or seeing him disappear into a vaguely determined heaven. Rather, the challenge consists in seeing both the world and heaven embodied in him: something new has begun; time and space are newly configured when the ascended Christ is the center and the focus of God's action and theological exploration.

A further effect of the ascension is to undermine idolatrous fixations and the hard lines of ideological positions. Jesus' departure as a visible worldly object makes room for a kind of unity in convergence and difference, since he is never to be contained or possessed as he departs from the world to which he will return as the fulfillment of history. For faith to ascend with him into the realm of the Father, there is a moment of openness to indefinably divine horizons. A homogenized sameness, the flat routine of taken for granted religious propositions uttered without any sense of depth or height, even ecclesial institutions untroubled by the absence or prospective return of the ascended Christ, to say nothing of the timidity of cosmic hope in any age, are all called into question. A flat ideology of uniformity undermines the experience of the vertically-given new, as if the transcendent Christ is to be converted to *us*, rather than *we* being converted to the radically new of the ascended One in an open-ended communal history.

A refreshed sense of Christ as the transcendent and indefinably all-inclusive Other is a powerful stimulus to dialogue. In the wide world of divine creation, and in the boundless dimensions of God's heaven to which Christ has ascended, he is not contained but adored and named as the Lord of all creation to the glory of the Father (Phil 2:10-11). Unconstrained by any mundane condition, Christ must be left free to act and to give in ways always hidden to human comprehension. He is ascended.

Admittedly, dialogue in an interfaith or interreligious context can give the impression that the faith and religion concerned are fixed and finished entities, each a body of religious positions with clearly defined boundaries, doctrines, classic texts, and so forth, which those involved in dialogue speak "about." While it would be destructive to suggest that such dialogue must demand that those involved should hold their beliefs in suspension, it may prove more realistic to refer to "inter-hope" dialogue in a horizon opened up by the ascension. Dialogue would appear as an eschatological overture that brings a larger sense of proportion to the exchange, and makes for a more engaged and hopeful style of communication. The attitude of Christians engaged in dialogue with those of other faiths could be expressed in such words as, "I hope to share eternal life, in a transformed creation already anticipated in the risen and ascended Christ, with *you*, and all peoples as the beneficiaries of a limitless love, and destined to see God face to face." At the very least, such a hopeful, ascension-affected attitude would suggest something wonderfully indefinable, a horizon of excess and unimaginable possibilities, despite the force of present religious, spiritual, or philosophical differences.[24] Dialogue will always mean affirming the existence of the other in the sincerity of their convictions, their personal goodness, and their dedication to the absolute truth and good. But it also means a readiness to share what is most precious and liberating for ourselves, to share what is destined for all in the infinite possibilities of God's most abundant giving already anticipated in risen and ascended Christ.

After sketching some of the elements that must figure in a theology of the ascension, we are in a position to offer some concluding reflections on where they might lead.

[24] See Anthony J. Kelly, *Eschatology and Hope* (Maryknoll, NY: Orbis Books, 2006), 15–17, 25–28.

Chapter 8

"Lift Up Your Hearts"
Looking in the Right Direction

To conclude this brief theology of the ascension and to emphasize once more its relevance to the life of faith, a number of comments suggest themselves. Necessarily, they follow the direction of Paul's words, "forgetting what lies behind and straining forward to what lies ahead, I press on toward the goal for the prize of the heavenly call of God in Christ Jesus" (Phil 3:13-14). Today, however, anyone sharing the apostle's eagerness "to press on toward the goal" cannot but be affected by the mood of hesitation and disillusionment characteristic of this historical period. It is often referred to as a "postmodern" era—a suitable tag to evoke the disconcerting fluidity in the ways of thinking and living in an increasingly complex world. "Postmodern" obviously means a period coming after what is assumed to be the solid style and clear certainties of the lengthy "modern" era. In this regard, it suggests a slippage from the classical forms of philosophy, theology, art, and even social and political organization.

The classic forms which shaped the formative traditions informing the modern world up to the present were held in place by implicit philosophical commitments. There were shared assumptions concerning the nature of reality, the human person, the human capacity to know, the existence of God, values of religion, beauty, and virtue. But a great change has taken place. Opinions may well differ in describing the present situation or in diagnosing its problems. But all agree that this is a changing world. Consequently, the church, being part of that world, is not spared exposure to the seismic shifts that have occurred in human and historical experience.

In this postmodern context, the *sursum corda* of the ascension invites faith to be bolder and more confident in its commitment to the distinctive character of Christian revelation, the sense of reality it communicates, and the moral conduct it inspires. When the shape of reality in all its guises has become so fluid, it is a good time to rise to the challenge of witnessing to the singular reality of the Christ Event, and to explore and communicate it in the largest hermeneutical and contemplative space—cosmic, ecumenical, interfaith, and eschatological. To that degree, the summons of *sursum corda* flowing from the ascension promotes a more creative catholicity. Essential Christian doctrines, flowing from and leading back to Christ, inevitably set hard in the particular forms and manners of expression typical of different times and their respective contacts—institutional, pastoral, moral, and so forth. But what is lacking in such particular contexts is the dimension of *sursum*—that "other dimension" in the ecology of faith—whether we choose to name it in terms of transcendence, open-ended otherness, singularity, awe, or mystery.

Caught up into the updraft of the ascension, Christian faith is drawn into the incalculable "more," into the inexhaustible excess of the mystery of God's self-giving in Christ. The particular manner of its appearance (i.e., its "phenomenality"), is inseparable from the free gift of the Spirit, on the one hand, and the promised but incalculable return of Christ in the fullness of his self-manifestation. In other words, the ascent of Christ from the empirical world of his previous existence is not a pure negation of sense, image, concept, or system. Though it certainly connotes a negation of time, place, accessibility, and previous forms of evidence, it is, theologically speaking, altogether positive in its connotation. The ascension determines the horizon of the communicative plenitude, the *pleroma* (in the Pauline sense), of Christ in all things, and all things in Christ—and of the community of faith drawn up and into that present reality.

While the ascension connotes fullness, plenitude, and completion of the mission of Christ, there is no reason to think of his ascended state in static terms—either for him, his followers, or for the universe itself. A more authentic reaction will envisage the time and space of the ascension of Christ as the realm of gifts—surprising, inexhaustible, and effective. The heaven of Christ's ascension is the realm from which the Spirit is given, along with the gifts of the Spirit forming the church. Further, as has been frequently mentioned, the era inaugurated in the ascension is one of promise and radical expectancy. Such a "lifting up of hearts" is not an invitation to enter some unworldly zone in which the humanity of Christ is dissolved or located in a "nowhere in particular," a universe radically alien to the bodily humanity we share with Christ. Rather, the church prays and hopes and awaits in faith for his return, for the full revelation and appearance of the crucified and risen One, Jesus of Nazareth. Consequently, the heaven to which he has ascended is not a terminal state of plenitude disallowing any future development and implying a terminal separation from the world he has left. It is a plenitude of promise for which there are no adequate words. The inexpressible particularity of this promise of Christ's return is based on the already realized supreme actuality of the resurrection, the first fruits of what will extend to all time, all people, and to the universe itself. What happened in Christ will happen for all as the Body of Christ grows to its full stature.

By focusing on the ascension of Christ, theology feels the need to keep a clear sense of the distinctive and singular character of Christian reality and its particular revelation. There is a singularity to be respected—the divine, freely chosen economy of God's self-revelation in this particular manner. It could have been otherwise—but this is how divine wisdom determined it—as enacted in Christ, and in his life, death, resurrection, ascension, in the outpouring of the Spirit, and in the promise of his return at the end of time.

We have already noted (in chapter 2) the multidimensional impact of the ascension on the life and imagination of the church through the images, symbols, narratives, and interpretations of the Christ Event expressed in the New Testament. From a Lukan perspective, the ascension is at once a looking back and a looking forward. It looks back in order to amplify faith's comprehension of the meaning of Jesus' life, mission, death, and resurrection. However, it also looks forward. The disciples are not left impotently gazing into the heavens, but looking outward into the life and mission of the church in its outreach to all peoples and all ages. As a result, Christian existence, retrospectively and prospectively, is deeply marked with the character of thanksgiving, waiting, and hope. Jesus has gone before us. But in the present time, the faith of his followers must now wait, longing for his return as the Lord and judge of all. Though no longer in the world as he was before, he is neither absent nor disengaged from it. The numinous cloud accompanies his departure and his promised return (Acts 1:9-11). But he is carried upward to this divine realm with arms extended in blessing (Luke 24:50-53)—a gesture of effective solidarity with all who will follow him (cf. Luke 22:42-43).

His departure in this way is a source of blessings and of the promised gift of the Spirit (Acts 1:6-8). In this sense, the ascension does not represent Jesus turning away from the community of faith, but rather an all-embracing turning to them from the height, depth, and breadth of the mystery of God.

With John the focus is less on the ascension as a discreet event and more on the action of the "ascending Jesus." Here as elsewhere in the New Testament and in every age of the church, the "ascended" state of Jesus is of the utmost relevance to the life of faith, always deriving from the transcendent identity of Christ: "No one has ascended into heaven except the one who descended from heaven, the Son of Man" (John 3:13). True faith lives from a particular vision, seeing "the Son of Man ascending to where he was before" (John 6:62)—an aspect of the "opened heaven" of communication between God and creation (John 1:51). In the two-way communication involved, not only does Jesus go to prepare a place for his followers, but he will also come again in order to gather them within the spacious hospitality of his Father's house (John 14:2-4).

The great prayer of Jesus (John 17) strikingly expresses the dynamic of the ascension of Jesus to the Father and its involvement of all who believe in him: "I glorified you on earth by finishing the work you gave me to do. So now, Father, glorify me in your own presence with the glory I had in your presence before the world existed" (John 17:4-5). The heavens are so opened (see John 1:51) as to enfold the world into that relationship that exceeds all created forms of belonging, namely the communion existing between the Father and his Son. As a result, though Jesus is going to the Father, the disciples will inhabit the world in a new way, as witnesses to what God is inviting the faithful to: "And now I am no longer in the world, but they are in the world, and I am coming to you" (John 17:11a). Jesus asks the Father to protect them so "that they may be one as we are one" (John 17:11b). In what his disciples already are, and through what they will later do, a new community based in the unity of the Father and the Son comes into being (John 17:20-21). Jesus prays that the disciples given to him by the Father will be transported into a new sphere of existence—to be where he is and to share in his vision and glory (John 17:24a).

The words of this prayer in the Gospel of John are not dealing with some distant existence in the future, but have immediate impact on Christian consciousness. By ascending to the Father and leaving the familiar world of his disciples, Jesus has in effect relocated them. Their world is changed. They live now in the heavenly realm of life and communion to which Christ has ascended, in the atmosphere of the Father's house of many dwelling places (John 14:2-3). The Father's original love for Jesus is now overflowing to those identified with him: "that the love with which you have loved me may be in them, and I in them" (17:26b). United with Jesus in his return to the Father, the disciples are drawn into the universe of mutual love and self-giving communion (John 13:34-35; 15:12, 17). It follows that not only is Jesus ascended, but also the disciples themselves are in a profound sense now "ascended" with him and share in his communion with the Father. By ascending to "my Father and your Father, to my God and your God" (John 20:17), the ascended and glorified Jesus both transcends all worldly realities, categories, and previous conceptions, and belongs to his follows in the deepest intimacy of his relationship to the Father.

Consequently, the ascension resonates in the consciousness of faith as an event (Luke-Acts) stimulating the mission of the church, and as a field of communion with the Father and the Son (John). From a Pauline perspective, the risen and ascended Christ is the source of gifts, building up the Body of Christ and bringing it to its fullest dimensions. After his self-emptying descent in lower parts of the earth, Christ ascends "above all heavens," not only that he might fill all things in a cosmic sense, but also that he might fill out the dimension of his Body with all the gifts necessary for its life, growth, and up-building in love (Eph 4:7-16)—even in the teeth of adverse cosmic powers (Eph 6:11-12). In Colossians, the apostle prays to the Father who has raised Jesus from the dead, who has "rescued us from the power of darkness and transferred us into the kingdom of his believed Son, in whom we have redemption, the forgiveness of sins" (Col 1:13-14). Once more it is clear that faith in God's action in Christ means a relocation of struggling Christian existence into the realm that Christ occupies, and in which he communicates present deliverance and forgiveness. The impact of the ascension of Christ on the consciousness of faith finds expression in the exhortation to "seek the things that are above, where Christ is, seated at the right hand of God" (Col 3:1). The believer is called beyond the limits of the mundane to the heights (v. 2). When life is transformed through Christ's death and resurrection, it is "hidden with Christ in God" (v.3) until its eventual glorious manifestation in him (Col 3:4). In the meantime, believers are clothed with the hidden reality of "the new self" (v.9). Thus, the "lift up your hearts" of the liturgy is a summons flowing directly from the confession of Christ's ascension.

The graphic symbolism of the Book of Revelation gives a dramatic emphasis to the activity of the risen and ascended Jesus—and the longing of the church for his return (Rev 22:20). In that respect, Jesus is the One who is to come (Rev 2:5, 16; 3:11; 16:15; 22:6, 12, 20). But at every stage and in every era, God rules the world through the Lamb who was slain (Rev 5:6), and, through him, brings about the salvation of the nations (Rev 15:3-4; 21:3). He is precisely identified as Jesus: "I was dead, and see I am alive forever and ever, and I have the keys of death and Hades" (Rev 1:18). The once dead and now living and reigning Christ invites believers into a new hope. The church longs for both the return of Jesus and the descent of the heavenly city as his bride (Rev 21:9). The course of history is to be judged from a heavenly perspective: Christ is not absent, but intensely present and active both in history and in the church.

By exploiting a range of temple symbolism, the Letter to Hebrews offers its particular vision of the ascended Jesus and his present relationship to Christian life. He is presented as the one who has gone before us, who has pierced the veil, and lives now in a state of uninterrupted intercession for all who are to follow him. The author of Hebrews—and the first generation of its readers—presume the exaltation of Jesus, along with his primordial and eschatological significance (see especially Heb 1:1-4). But there is a further element, namely, the intercessory activity of the ascended and glorified Jesus in heaven. This is described in terms of the high priestly Temple ritual: "Since, then, we have a great high priest who has passed through the heavens, Jesus, the Son of God, let us hold fast to our confession (Heb 4:14; cf. 7:26; 9:11-14). Christian faith follows Jesus to enter "the inner shrine behind the curtain, where Jesus, a forerunner on our behalf, has entered, having become a high priest forever according to the order of Melchizedek" (Heb 6:19-20). In his unique high priestly capacity, Jesus acts as the mediator of salvation, in solidarity with those who place their hope in him, "He is able for all time to save those who approach God through him, since he always lives to make intercession for them" (Heb 7:25). Not only is Jesus the Melchizedek-like high priestly intercessor, he exercises his ministry of salvation as one seated at the right hand of God: "we have such a high priest, one who is seated at the right hand of the throne of the

Majesty in the heavens" (Heb 8:1-2). From there he "will appear a second time, not to deal with sin, but to save those who are eagerly waiting for him" (Heb 9:27), to achieve ultimate victory over all opposition (Heb 10:12-13). In the meantime, he opens a "new and living way . . . through the curtain" (Heb 10:19) into the ultimate mystery of God.

In short, Jesus has passed through the veil, and now presides over the house of God and as God's right hand. There he acts as forerunner, representative, and intercessor for those who come after; from there, he will appear a second time. But even now his exaltation inspires a spiritual ascension of faith and hope in those who follow him (see Heb 10:19-25).

In every age, the ascension makes a difference to how faith understands Christ's communication with us, and ours with him. After these remarks on the significance of the ascension to Christian life, and following the reference to a number of representative instances of this in the New Testament, we can simply return to our starting point where we admitted that the ascension tends to be so implicit in the life and expression of faith that it passes practically, and even theoretically, unnoticed. I imagine it would be surprising to many that a whole treatise, however small, could be devoted to such a theme. But like all obvious and therefore, comparatively "taken for granted" matters, there is something of special importance, routinely hidden, to be freshly discovered there.

Admittedly, the ascension of Christ is not an abstract idea: it conveys something about Christ now and his presence to us in time and space—despite his absence from the world he inhabited two thousand years ago. Key passages in the New Testament suggest that in the ascension, Christ fills all things, places, and times with his presence. As a result, the faith of the church in every age and place has access to everything that he is in his life, death, and resurrection, everything he can give in terms of communicating the Spirit, and all that he will be in his promise to return at the ending of the age. In short, the ascension of Jesus means his immediate and effective presence to all the faithful through the whole of history.

For that very reason, a further remark is called for, especially if it is true that the ascension is the most taken for granted aspect of the mystery of Christ in the religious world in which Christians habitually live. Religious living and even Christian religious living can become flat and monodimensional. It might seem that life is being

lived in a plastic wrapper called "religion." A strange forgetfulness
threatens when habitual practices become merely routine. Words can
come too easily to the preacher; the missionary or pastoral planner
settles for the predictabilities of business as usual; and the range of
Christian sensibility is so effectively channeled into a yearly cycle
of feasts and other celebrations—especially at Christmas, Easter,
and the feasts of patron saints—that something essential is miss-
ing. However absurd it may sound, this familiar envelope of routine
religious life and Christian commitment can deaden our sensitivities to the infinite height and depth of the mystery of God—and of
human destiny in God.

True, we are only human beings, and the mercy of God has ac-
commodated itself to our human capacities. The Word became flesh,
God became man, and the incarnation is the focal doctrine of Christian faith. But even that great central and classic doctrine dampens
the freshness of our sense of God unless it is understood as an event
expanding to all its depths and heights—down into the darkness of
the death and burial of the crucified Jesus, into the dawning light of
his rising from the tomb, and up into the expanse of his ascent to
God from which he came. To put it most simply, the ascension leads
faith back to God as it contemplates Jesus now at the right hand of
the Father. The ascension draws faith into the realm that is proper to
God, and that only Christ can occupy. In all this, faith is not a neatly
packaged addition to ordinary life, nor is it an expression of human
ambition and control. It is an open surrender, in and through Christ,
to the infinities of God's love, grace, mercy, and beauty. A continual
alertness is necessary if faith is not to lose its self-transcending character by creating an attractive idol in Christian clothing. Faith moves
with Christ ever upward, outward, and beyond itself to the realm of
the Father. God is not like anything in the world, and the kingdom
of God surpasses the projections of human imagination and ambi-
tions of human control and calculation.

Inevitably, it must seem to those deeply affected by the plight of
the world's poor that thinking about the ascension is a grand distraction, even more than the resurrection itself.[1] On the other hand, the

[1] See Anthony J. Kelly, *The Resurrection Effect*, in its treatment of "The Resurrection and Moral Theology," 159–167, and "Beyond Locked Doors: The Breath
of the Risen One," in *Violence, Desire and the Sacred: Girard's Mimetic Theory
Across the Disciplines*, ed. Scott Cowdell, Chris Fleming, and Joel Hodge (New York:

exaltation of the crucified One to the right hand of the Father, whom all creation must acknowledge as Lord, must have consequences for our way of looking at the world as it is and for our way of treating those who are most disadvantaged and victimized within it. If social action on behalf of the poor loses its eschatological sense of direction, if it shrinks the horizon of loving the neighbor to a very particular ideology, it is deprived of the oxygen of its sense of God and of hope for the world.

The atmosphere of Christian faith and hope is strikingly expressed in John's gospel. The risen (and ascended) Jesus appears to his disciples huddled in their fear-locked room. After greeting them with peace, he points them beyond the walls of the room to that larger world of mission: "As the Father has sent me, so I send you" (John 20:21). He then breathes on them and says, "Receive the Holy Spirit" (John 20:22). With the "holy breath" of the risen One, believers inhale the new atmosphere of the Spirit. With fresh energy they can enter the world, witness to the gift of God, and resist the enslaving power of the world from which Jesus has ascended. Conformity to the self-enclosed world that Christ has left has no future, whereas the faithful who go with Christ into the realm of God anticipate the fullness of life: "The world and its desire is passing away, but those who do the will of God live forever" (1 John 2:17). The Spirit breathed forth by the risen and ascended Christ detoxifies the noxious culture of conformity, and witnesses to the present source and form of true life (cf. John 16:8-11).

The "advantage" the disciples are to enjoy cannot be appreciated by those still in the undisturbed world of distorted desires (John 14:17). Only when that world is shaken out of its self-enclosure by the departure of Jesus and the consequent sending of the Spirit of truth can the significance of Jesus leaving the world be appreciated. His departure is not one more grief added to the sum of the world's sorrows, but the condition for the reception of the gift that will make all the difference to the disciples' experience of what true life can mean. When Jesus is lifted up on the cross and glorified by the Father in his self-giving love, he will draw all to himself (John 12:32-33). In this respect, the Paraclete is the crowning glory of Jesus' mission,

---

Continuum, 2012), 69–85; More extensively, see Brian D. Robinette, *Grammars of Resurrection: A Christian Theology of Presence and Absence* (New York: Crossroad, 2009), 227–90.

bringing home to the disciples all that Jesus is and calls to. For this reason, the Advocate is sent to fill the void that Jesus' absence will create in the seemingly triumphant world that brought about his death. But the coming of the Spirit is not just a remedy for Jesus' absence, nor a sedative for the disciples' suffering. For this Spirit is given to bring about the fulfillment to which everything is moving, once the Son has come into the world: "as the Father has sent me, so I send you" (John 20:21). His ascension to the Father occurs as the overture to space and time of mission—which is to be conducted in the energy and under the guidance of the Spirit.

The conclusion of John's gospel reminds believers of every age that Christian faith is not a verbal formula of belief, nor even a particular program of action. The crucified and risen One has appeared in the fear-locked room of the disciples to breathe the Spirit on them and send them forth on mission. The ascended Jesus is present to all disciples in their "fear-locked rooms" in every age. He comes into those places of dejection to send forth his followers, and to breathe into them the Spirit. This ongoing, inexhaustible event of his death, resurrection, and ascension is not contained within the linear script of any book—nor in the sum total of all the books of the world (John 21:25). Christ's ascension to the Father means that his presence and action cannot be confined or restricted. It invites believers always "upward," and into this "other dimension."

Selected Bibliography

Alison, James. *Raising Abel: The Recovery of the Eschatological Imagination*. New York: Crossroads, 1996.

Balthasar, Hans Urs von. *Mysterium Paschale: The Mystery of Easter*. Translated with an introduction by Aidan Nichols. Edinburgh: T&T Clark, 1990.

———. *The Glory of the Lord: A Theological Aesthetics*. Vol. 1: *Seeing the Form*. Edited by Joseph Fessio and John Riches. Translated by Erasmo Leiva-Merikakis. Edinburgh: T. & T. Clark, 1982.

———. *The Glory of the Lord: A Theological Aesthetics*. Vol. 7: *Theology: The New Covenant*. Edited by Joseph Fessio and John Riches. Translated by Brian McNeil. Edinburgh: T. & T. Clark, 1989.

———. *Theo-drama: Theological Dramatic Theory*. Vol. 3: *Dramatis Personae: Persons in Christ*. Translated by Graham Harison. San Francisco: Ignatius Press, 1992.

———. *Theo-drama: Theological Dramatic Theory*. Vol.5: *The Last Act*. Translated by Graham Harison. San Francisco: Ignatius Press, 1998.

———. *Theo-logic: Theological Logical Theory*. Vol. 5: *The Spirit of Truth*. Translated by Graham Harison. San Francisco: Ignatius Press, 2005.

———. *A Theology of History*. San Francisco: Ignatius Press, 1994.

Barth, Karl. *Church Dogmatics*. Vol. 4. Edited by G. W. Bromiley and T. F. Torrance. Edinburgh: T. & T. Clark, 1956–77.

Bobrinskoy, Boris. "Worship and the Ascension of Christ," *Studia Liturgica* 2 (1963): 108–123.

Bulgakov, Sergius. *The Lamb of God*. Translated by Boris Jakim. Grand Rapids, MI: Eerdmans, 2008.

Coloe, Mary. *God Dwells with Us: Temple Symbolism in the Fourth Gospel*. Collegeville, MN: Liturgical Press, 2001.

Davies, J. G. *He Ascended into Heaven: A Study in the History of Doctrine*. London: Lutterworth Press, 1958.

Davies, Oliver, Paul D. Janz, and Clemens Sedmak, *Transformation Theology: Churches in the World*. New York: T. & T. Clark, 2007.

Davis, Stephen T., Daniel Kendall, and Gerald O'Collins, eds. *The Resurrection: An Interdisciplinary Symposium on the Resurrection of Jesus*. New York: Oxford University Press, 1997.

Donne, Brian K. "The Significance of the Ascension of Jesus in the New Testament." *Scottish Journal of Theology* 30 (1977): 555–68.

Durrwell, F. X. *The Resurrection: A Biblical Study*. Translated by Rosemary Sheed. London and New York: Sheed and Ward, 1960.

———. *The Eucharist: Presence of Christ*. Translated by S. Attanasio. Denville, NJ: Dimension Books, 1974.

———. *L'eucharistie: Sacrement Pascal*. Paris: Cerf, 1980.

Farrow, Douglas. *Ascension and Ecclesia: on the Significance of the Doctrine of the Ascension for Ecclesiology and Christian Cosmology*. Edinburgh: T. & T. Clark, 1999.

———. *Ascension Theology*. London: T. & T. Clark International, 2011.

———. "Karl Barth on the Ascension: An Appreciation and Critique." *International Journal of Systematic Theology* 2, no. 2 (July 2000): 127–50.

Fitzmyer, J. A. "The Ascension of Christ and Pentecost." *Theological Studies* 45 (1984): 409–40.

Gavrilyuk, Paul, and Sarah Coakley, eds. *The Spiritual Senses: Perceiving God in Western Christianity*. Cambridge, UK: Cambridge University Press, 2012.

Geerlings, Wilhelm. "Ascensio Christi." In *Augustinus* Lexikon 1. Edited by Petrus C. Mayer. Basel: Schwabe Verlag, 1986–1994.

Granados, José. "The First Fruits of the Flesh and the First Fruits of the Spirit: The Mystery of the Ascension." *Communio* 38, no. 1 (Spring 2011): 6–38.

Hart, David Bentley. *The Beauty of the Infinite: The Aesthetics of Christian Truth*. Grand Rapids, MI: Eerdmans, 2003.

Hart, Kevin, ed. *Counter-Experiences: Reading Jean-Luc Marion*. Notre Dame, IN: University of Notre Dame Press, 2007.

Haught, John F. *Christianity and Science: Toward a Theology of Nature*. Maryknoll, NY: Orbis Books, 2007.

Heaney, Maeve Louise. *Music as Theology: What Music Says about the Word*. Eugene, OR: Pickwick Publications, 2012.

Henry, Michel. *Incarnation. Une philosophie de la chair*. Paris: Seuil, 2000.

Horner, Robyn. *Rethinking God as Gift: Marion, Derrida and the Limits of Phenomenology*. New York: Fordham University Press, 2001.

———. *Jean-Luc Marion: A Theo-Logical Introduction*. Burlington, VT: Ashgate, 2005.

Hunt, Anne. *The Trinity and the Paschal Mystery: A Development in Recent Catholic Theology*. Collegeville, MN: Liturgical Press, 1997.

———. *Trinity: Nexus of the Mysteries of Christian Faith*. Maryknoll, NY: Orbis Books, 2005.

———. "The Psychological Analogy and the Paschal Mystery in Trinitarian Theology." *Theological Studies* 59 (1998): 197–218.

Johnson, Luke Timothy. *The Acts of the Apostles*. Sacra Pagina 5. College-
ville, MN: Liturgical Press, 1992.
———. *The Gospel of Luke*. Sacra Pagina 3. Collegeville, MN: Liturgical
Press, 1991.
Kapic, Kelly M., and Wesley Vander Lugt. "The Ascension of Jesus and the
Descent of the Holy Spirit in Patristic Perspective: A Theological Read-
ing." *Evangelical Quarterly* 79, no. 1 (2007): 23–33.
Kasper, Walter. "Christi Himmelfahrt: Geschichte und theologische Be-
deutung." *Internationale katholische Zeitschrift Communio* 12 (1983):
205–13.
Kelly, Anthony J. *The Bread of God: Nurturing a Eucharistic Imagination*.
Melbourne: HarperCollins Religious, 2001.
———. *Eschatology and Hope*. Maryknoll, NY: Orbis Books, 2006.
———. *The Resurrection Effect: Transforming Christian Life and Thought*.
Maryknoll, NY: Orbis Books, 2008.
———. "Refreshing Experience: The Christ-Event as Fact, Classic, and
Phenomenon," *Irish Theological Quarterly* 77, no. 4 (November 2012):
335–48.
Kelly, Anthony J., and Francis J. Moloney. *Experiencing God in the Gospel
of John*. Mahwah, NJ: Paulist Press, 2003.
Kendal, Daniel, and Stephen T. Davis, eds. *The Convergence of Theology:
A Festschrift Honoring Gerald O'Collins, SJ*. Mahwah, NJ: Paulist Press,
2001.
Lacoste, Jean-Yves. *Experience and the Absolute: Disputed Questions on
the Humanity of Man*. Translated by Mark Raftery-Skehan. New York:
Fordham University Press, 2004.
Lohfink, Gerhard. *Die Himmelfahrt Jesu: Untersuchungen zu den Himmel-
fahrts-und Erhohungstexten bei Lukas*. Studien zom Alten und Neuen
Testament 26. Munich: Kösel-Verlag, 1971.
Mackinlay, Shane. *Interpreting Excess: The Implicit Hermeneutics of Jean-
Luc Marion's Saturated Phenomena*. Leuven: Katholieke Universiteit
Leuven. Hoger Instituut voor Wijsbegeerte, 2004.
Marion, Jean-Luc, *God without Being: Hors-Texte*. Translated by Thomas
A. Carlson. Chicago: University of Chicago Press, 1991.
———. "The Saturated Phenomenon." In *Phenomenology and the "Theo-
logical Turn": The French Debate*. Dominique Janicaud et al. Translated
by Thomas A. Carlson. New York: Fordham University Press, 2000.
———. *The Idol and Distance: Five Studies*. Translated by Thomas A.
Carlson. New York: Fordham University Press, 2001.
———. *In Excess: Studies of Saturated Phenomena*. Translated by Robyn
Horner and Vincent Barraud. New York: Fordham University Press, 2002.
———. *The Crossing of the Visible*. Translated by James K. A. Smith. Stan-
ford, CA: Stanford University Press, 2004.

Martelet, G. *The Risen Christ and the Eucharistic World*. Translated by René Hague. New York: Seabury Press, 1976.

Moloney, Francis J. *The Gospel of John*. Sacra Pagina 4. Collegeville, MN: Liturgical Press, 1998.

Muldowney, Mary Sarah, trans. *Saint Augustine: Sermons on the Liturgical Seasons*. New York: Fathers of the Church. Inc., 1959.

Nancy, Jean-Luc. *Au fond des images*. Paris: Editions Galilée, 2003.

O'Collins, Gerald. *Believing in the Resurrection: the Meaning and Promise of the Risen Jesus*. Mahwah, NJ: Paulist Press, 2012.

Pannenberg, Wolfhart. *Systematic Theology*. Vol. 3. Translated by Geoffrey W. Bromiley. Edinburgh: T. & T. Clark, 1993.

Ratzinger, Joseph Cardinal. *The Spirit of the Liturgy*. Translated by Johan Saward. San Francisco: Ignatius Press, 2000.

Robinette, Brian D. *Grammars of Resurrection: A Christian Theology of Presence and Absence*. Crossroad: New York, 2009.

Sleeman, Matthew. *Geography and the Ascension Narrative in Acts*. New York: Cambridge University Press, 2009.

Sokolowski, Robert. *Introduction to Phenomenology*. Cambridge, UK: Cambridge University Press, 2000.

Steinbock, Anthony J. *Phenomenology and Mysticism: The Verticality of Religious Experience*. Bloomington and Indianapolis: Indiana University Press, 2009.

Torrance, Thomas F. *Space, Time and Resurrection*. Edinburgh: T. & T. Clark, 1976 (pb. 1998).

Index